	DATE DUE		

FRONTIER
MERCHANTS

FRONTIER MERCHANTS

Lionel and Barron Jacobs
and the Jewish Pioneers
Who Settled the West

by Jerry Stanley

ILLUSTRATED WITH PHOTOGRAPHS

CROWN PUBLISHERS, INC., NEW YORK

Published by Crown Publishers, Inc., a Random House company,
201 East 50th Street,
New York, New York 10022

CROWN is a trademark of Crown Publishers, Inc.

Printed in the United States of America

www.randomhouse.com/kids

Library of Congress Cataloging-in-Publication Data
Frontier Merchants: Lionel & Barron Jacobs and the Jewish Pioneers Who Settled the West;
Jerry Stanley.
Includes biographical references.
Summary: Tells the story of Lionel and Barron Jacobs, Jewish merchants who started with a general store in Tucson in 1867 and went on to found Arizona's first bank.
1. Jacobs, Lionel, 1840–1922—Juvenile literature.
2. Jacobs, Barron, 1846–1936—Juvenile literature.
3. Tucson (Ariz.)—Biography—Juvenile literature.
4. Frontier and pioneer life—Arizona—Tucson—Juvenile literature.
5. Merchants, Jewish—Arizona—Tucson—Biography—Juvenile literature.
6. Jews—Arizona—Tucson—Biography—Juvenile literature.
7. Pioneers—Arizona—Tucson—Biography—Juvenile literature.
[1. Jacobs, Lionel, 1840–1922. 2. Jacobs, Barron, 1846–1936. 3. Frontier and pioneer life—Arizona.
4. Jews—Arizona—Biography. 5. Arizona—Biography.] I. Title.
F819.T953J337   1998
979.1'77604'092—dc21
[B]

ISBN   0-517-80019-5 (trade)
0-517-80020-9 (lib. bdg.)

10 9 8 7 6 5 4 3 2 1

First Edition

For Mom

Contents

Introduction 1

One: The Road to San Bernardino 5

Two: The Gila Trail 12

Three: The Smell of Mesilla 21

Four: Stern-Wheelers, Four-Inchers,
and the Nigh 31

Five: The Shoo Fly Feeling 41

Six: Fifty Cigars and Perfumy 51

Seven: The Money Game 61

Eight: The Goodness of the Heart 70

Nine: The Goodness of Life 79

Afterword 90
Bibliographic Note 95
Index 99

FRONTIER
MERCHANTS

Introduction

On January 24, 1848, James W. Marshall was building a sawmill on the American River in northern California when he spotted several gleaming nuggets of gold just below the water's surface. Marshall tried to keep the discovery a secret, but word leaked out and by 1849 gold fever had struck the United States and much of the world. It was said, "The blacksmith dropped his hammer, the carpenter his plane, the baker his loaf, and the drunkard his bottle." Thousands of people headed west for a chance at instant fortune. The result was the California gold rush, which hastened the settlement of the Far West.

At the time of Marshall's discovery, the western third of the United States was home to more than a million Native Americans, but only a handful of whites had settled in the region. Stretching from the western border of Kansas to the Pacific Ocean, the West of 1848 was populated by a few thousand Mormons in Utah, a few thousand pioneers in Oregon and California, and a scattering of mountain men, drifters, and thieves who lived outside of the law and society. Fewer than twenty thousand whites lived west of Kansas, and less than three thousand Americans lived in California. Marshall's discovery of gold changed all this: By 1860, California had a population of three hundred thousand, and other communities had been started in Colorado, Wyoming, Arizona, and New Mexico.

The people who participated in the settlement of the West were of every character and type. Besides gold seekers, farmers came to grow food, ranchers to raise cattle, saloon keepers to pour whiskey, and fast-talking men in cheap suits to sell "goldometers," "guaranteed" to find hidden wealth. Journalists came. Politicians came. Carpenters, masons, and ministers came. Women came as wives and daughters and as independent individuals seeking a better life.

The people who moved west starting in 1849 came from all over the world and from a variety of racial backgrounds. By 1860, 80 percent of California's population was foreign-born, with Mexicans, Germans, French, and Irish predominating. The population included 4,086 African Americans and some 35,000 Asians. These same groups settled in other new communities in the West and were joined by Scots, Dutch, Italians, and Swedes. They were farmers, ranchers, blacksmiths, and tailors, and they often switched jobs to get ahead. Their story is the story of ordinary people who worked very hard, mostly prospered, and helped build the West.

Among them was another pioneer, one who has often been overlooked in the settlement of the West. Imagine him on almost any frontier wearing a businessman's hat, a pocket watch, and a suit in need of cleaning. There he was, bouncing up and down in a wagon carrying canned goods, coffee, whiskey, and flour and choking on the dust kicked up by his team of mules. He never received the fame of the mountain man or the Indian fighter, but in his own way he was a hero in the settlement of the West, for without him settlement wouldn't have been possible. He sold the mountain man his traps and the Indian fighter his bullets—and he sold seeds, barbed wire, branding irons, and plows. He was the pioneer merchant.

During the California gold rush, pioneer merchants supplied the goods that other migrants needed so they could mine gold, start farms, and establish other businesses. With their life savings or a loan from a bank, they bought wagons and hauled goods to the mining areas, selling beans, rough clothes, and broad felt hats for ounces of gold dust. To succeed they had to know the exact value of each item, the cost of transporting it, and where they might sell the item and for how much. To succeed they had to drive their wagons for ten hours a day through rivers and over crude roads with chuckholes that could snap off a wagon wheel and damage the stock of goods. They had to ensure that they had enough food in the wagon for the team of mules, and they had to know where the team could get water. Bandits, flash floods, and severe storms also occupied their minds, as well as competition from other merchants with better goods at lower prices.

Many of these merchants were Jewish, and they played an important role in the gold rush and the settlement of the West. Between 1847 and 1860, approximately 100,000 Jews emigrated from Europe to America, and by the mid-1870s, 21,257 had settled in the region west of Kansas. Like other migrants, the Jewish pioneers pursued a variety of occupations in the West. In California, Levi Strauss sold jeans and jackets, and in Cheyenne, Wyoming, Henry Altman raised cattle. In Denver, Colorado, Simon Fishman grew wheat, and in Santa Cruz, Arizona, Leopold Ephraim built hotels.

Jews panned gold, planted corn, and played poker, but the Jewish pioneers were most prominent as merchants. For centuries, trading had been the traditional occupation for the Jews of Europe, who were excluded from farming and other occupations because of their religion. With news of the California gold rush, they put their skill at selling to work. Perhaps half of all Jews in the Far West were merchants, and it has been estimated that they conducted nearly half of the merchandising business in the western states before 1900.

When the California gold rush ended in 1860, and even before, some of the Jewish merchants, with other merchants who weren't Jewish, packed their wagons with beans and flour and headed east. Almost unnoticed, the wagons arrived in places that would eventually become Boise in Idaho, Billings in Montana, Carson City in Nevada, and Phoenix in Arizona. The western towns acquired a distinctive look with the arrival of the merchants, who usually wore suits and hats and displayed good manners, unlike many of the townspeople. On the dusty trails leading to the towns, they tipped their hats to strangers and smiled with dirt on their teeth. The blistering sun turned the backs of their hands red as they held the reins that guided the mules steady. Past rattlesnakes, scorpions, and packs of wolves, they drove their wagons into the desert and helped build new communities. Among them were Lionel and Barron Jacobs, the adventurous sons of Mark Israel Jacobs.

ONE

The Road to San Bernardino

Mark Israel Jacobs was born in Poland in 1816 to a family of impoverished street peddlers. When Mark was twelve, his father inherited a small sum of money and moved the family to England, where he opened a clothing store and taught Mark the business of selling. In 1840, at the age of twenty-four, Mark married Hannah Soloman and afterward moved his family to Baltimore, Maryland, where he operated a clothing store for seven years. In 1851, at the height of the gold rush, he moved to California and established a merchandising business in San Diego. Mark and Hannah had twelve children. Lionel, the third, was born in 1840, and Barron, the fifth, in 1846.

Lionel and Barron spent their childhood years in San Diego, then a community of less than a thousand people. The brothers attended school together, and when Lionel was fourteen and Barron eight, they earned pocket money by working as bee-keepers, repairing the wooden hives and harvesting the honey. According to their mother, Barron showed an interest in the business and the behavior of bees, but Lionel did not. He was careless and was often stung while rushing to complete the work as quickly as possible.

The brothers sometimes skipped school for a day at the beach, where Lionel taught Barron how to swim. When they were caught skipping school, they were paddled by their father and lectured on the importance of education. For centuries in Europe, Mark's ancestors had been denied an education, which had kept them in poverty. Mark's own father could barely write, and he had been strict with Mark's education in England. Eventually the brothers took an interest in learning. At the age of fifteen, Lionel was studying bookkeeping and pursuing a hobby of public speaking. He helped establish the San Diego Lyceum and Debating Club and served as its first secretary.

In 1859, Mark moved the family north to San Bernardino after Leah, his firstborn, married a Jewish immigrant and moved there. San Bernardino had a population of fifteen hundred, among whom the Jewish population numbered about fifty. It was a stopping point for migrants headed to the goldfields, and business was brisk in supplying travelers with clothing, food, and lodging. Mark and a business partner managed two stores and a hotel. In 1860, Mark consolidated his operations and established the Mark Jacobs Company, a general-merchandising store with assets of approximately ten thousand dollars.

Lionel joined the business in 1861 at the age of twenty-one, and Barron became an employee the following year. At the time, Lionel was described as six feet tall and lanky but neat in appearance and dress. He favored the outdoors and physical activities such as swimming and running, and he was popular with girls. Barron was five feet ten and stocky. He had an interest in most everything, especially reading and world geography. Lionel was talkative and outgoing; Barron was more the silent type. Barron took a serious approach to most things; Lionel was a joker. While clerking in their father's store, they quarreled over lost receipts and whose turn it was to sweep the floor. Otherwise, they were close and spent a lot of time together, which pleased their father, who had been an only child.

While learning the merchandising business in San Bernardino, Lionel and Barron also learned about prejudice toward Jews. Their sister Jane had married Wolff Cohn, a Jewish immigrant from Prussia. Wolff Cohn operated a dry-goods store in San Bernardino. On the afternoon of January 2, 1862, a drunken desperado named Dick Cole entered Cohn's store and started a fight over a pair of boots. Cole pushed Cohn and called him "a damn Jew son of a bitch." After exchanging punches, Cole drew a handgun and fired, killing Lionel and Barron's brother-in-law. In a letter to a relative in San Francisco, Lionel described the murder as "an act of hate." "There are those who hate the Jew," he said, "because they have been taught to hate the Jew. We have learned, however, that the popular view is one of acceptance."

Lionel was right. Following Cohn's murder, fear spread through the San Bernardino Jewish community, and Jewish businesses were put up for sale. But the town's population rallied behind the merchants and persuaded most to stay. "We are determined to defend the lives and property of all of our citizens," a newspaper editor wrote. "We will not allow a certain class of individuals to drive out of our community the most respectable elements in the community." Later, when Cohn's brother shot Cole dead, a grand jury refused to indict him. The jury ruled: "Rowdyism has been taught a lesson. It cannot ride roughshod over respectable members of society."

Elsewhere in the West, Jews occasionally experienced anti-

Semitism, laws and practices that discriminated against Jews. The Jewish sabbath was on Saturday; the Christian sabbath was on Sunday. While Christian businessmen operated on Saturday, some towns passed "Sunday laws" prohibiting businesses from operating on Sunday—specifically, Jewish businesses. In the nineteenth century, it was a common practice of Dun & Company, a powerful credit-rating firm, to give a poor credit rating to a person identified as a "Jew" or "Hebrew," considering such people untrustworthy. But Jews were no better or worse than other businessmen, and those who were honest in business easily established credit.

What made the Jewish experience in the West stand out was how well Jews were accepted. Jewish temples stood next to Protestant churches and were not so different in appearance. Jews worked side by side with other groups, and individuals did not make their private faith a matter of public display. As Mark Jacobs said about the Mormons in San Bernardino, "I extend the same toleration to the Mormons that I claim for myself, and however much I differ from them on matters of faith, I respect them for believing what to them are sacred truths."

Mark stayed in San Bernardino and the Mark Jacobs Company prospered. With his sons-in-law, Mark established the San Bernardino Hebrew and English Academy, the first Jewish day school in the West. Along with other siblings, Lionel and Barron continued working in the store, but by the time Barron was in his early twenties, even he was bored with the work. "I hope to do something on my own some day," he wrote to a former classmate in San Diego, "something besides stacking boxes and counting receipts." Lionel had been restless even longer. The only event they looked forward to was traveling with their father to San Francisco on buying trips.

One drawback for a young Jewish man in San Bernardino was the lack of young Jewish women—or any women, for that matter—and privacy was difficult with a mother and nosy sisters nearby. San Francisco was a big city with women of every kind, and during buying trips the brothers took pleasure in their free time. They would disappear for two days at a time, and upon their return Mark acted as if they had been gone for two hours. The brothers also acquired a taste for fine foods and imported wines in the eating establishments they were introduced to by their father.

San Francisco, 1865.

Lionel and Barron's chance for independence came in the form of a brief news item in the *San Francisco Chronicle* of April 10, 1867. Easily overlooked as unimportant, the item caught the eye of a man who was looking to make more money and who had two sons in need of a future. Mark read that the military headquarters in the Arizona Territory was to be moved from Prescott, in the central part of the territory, to Tucson, located sixty miles north of the Mexican border. In addition, the territorial capital was to be relocated from Prescott to Tucson. The move was scheduled for November 1. Tucson was in Pima County, which had a population of 2,776 and was the largest county in the Arizona Territory. Mark calculated that its population would double with the arrival of the soldiers and government workers. If a merchant could establish a business there, the chances of making money were good.

Mark explained the opportunity to his sons and offered to back them financially if they would go to Tucson and start a business. Lionel and Barron accepted the offer without hesitation, although neither had experience as a frontier merchant and neither had traveled through the desert before. Nor had they suffered real hardship in life. These facts were apparently unimportant when compared with the chance of independence and wealth. "Once we get the business going," Barron wrote to a friend in San Diego, "we will receive a share of the profits, which will be ours to use as we wish." Lionel wrote, "We leave for Tucson in the Arizona Territory, where Barron and I are to start a business with our father's blessing and money. We anticipate nothing but success." At the time, Lionel was twenty-seven and Barron was twenty-one.

In less than two weeks, Mark had purchased the items needed for the trip: a team of twelve mules fitted with harnesses and bits and a freight wagon that was four feet deep, five feet wide, and twenty feet long. The brothers packed some personal possessions in the wagon—shirts, an extra pair of boots, soap—then loaded the wagon full of canned goods—approximately twelve hundred cans, each the size of a soup can. When they climbed into the wagon and sat in the buckboard seat, Lionel and Barron were dressed in business suits and hats. They waved as they slapped the reins against the mules and pulled away, but there were no long good-byes because they were in partnership with their father and would see him again. For now the task at hand was to make a trip of more than four hundred miles through unfamiliar land to a place called Tucson in the Arizona Territory.

TWO

The Gila Trail

Lionel and Barron left San Bernardino in mid-May 1867 and headed south to San Diego, the takeoff point for the Gila Trail across southern California to Arizona. They did not stay long in the place where they had grown up. Although they had only a vague idea of where they were going, they knew about the extreme heat in the desert, and it was not their wish to become a meal for a flock of hungry buzzards. At an average rate of twenty miles a day, they figured they would reach Tucson in four weeks, by mid-June, avoiding the blast-furnace heat of July and August. Staying only long enough to load the wagon with twenty five-gallon tins of water, Lionel and Barron headed into the desert to make a new life for themselves.

Their first challenge came just outside of San Diego, when they encountered the Laguna Mountains. Starting at sea level with a gentle upward slope, the mountains eventually rose to more than 6,300 feet. Some of the steep passes stretched for three miles at a thirty-degree angle, and as the brothers struggled against the steep grades, their wagon resembled a roller-coaster car creeping into the sky. On the trip downward they had to pull on the hand brake with all their might to avoid becoming a roller-coaster car out of control. It was hard on the mules and hard on the drivers: three hours of upgrade followed by two hours of downgrade when one slip could send the wagon over the cliff. Barron reflected his and Lionel's cheerless sentiments in a journal he kept for a report to their father. "The temperature is mild," he wrote, "but that is the only good thing about these mountains. We did not foresee their expanse, and they are a curse to anyone who thinks they are easily conquered." The brothers figured on averaging twenty miles a day. It took twelve days to cross the mountains at an average rate of three miles a day.

Once past the mountains, Lionel and Barron averaged less than six miles a day through the southern Mojave Desert. In August, this ninety-mile stretch of sand and brush was an oven, where most living things hid during the day to escape the heat. But at the end of May, when Lionel and Barron started into the area, the land was a floodplain for the spring rains of the desert. On some days no travel was possible as miles of racing water obliterated every sign of the trail. More than once, Barron recorded, "We had to go backward through the mud to higher ground to keep from being swept away. . . . We are forced to stay under a tarp, where we eat a meal of hardtack and beans and wait for the water to recede, that being all we can do." It went on this way day after day—seven miles forward and two miles back, with the wagon sinking in the mud. They lost two mules to the floods and a wagon wheel was smashed by debris in the rushing water. But, Barron wrote, "No cargo was lost, so we continue on, wet and muddy like the mules."

The distance between San Diego and Fort Yuma on the Colorado River was some 170 miles. It took five weeks to reach Fort Yuma—not one week, as planned—and by then tempera-

Fort Yuma, about 1870.

tures were in the nineties. The soldiers stationed at the fort greeted the brothers as they chugged through the gate. They rested there two days. They ate hot meals, washed their clothes, washed the mules and the wagon, and separated their canned goods from the mud. They contracted with the operator of a ferryboat for the trip across the Colorado River and reached Arizona with one week left in June. They still had two thirds of the trip ahead of them, 235 miles from Fort Yuma to Tucson.

Lionel and Barron picked up the trail that ran alongside the Gila River where it intersected with the Colorado River. The trail ran northeast for approximately one hundred miles to Gila Bend, then veered southeast to Tucson, straight through the heart of the Sonoran Desert, where the sand turned menacingly red, as if to announce *"Stay Out!"*

Capable of reaching a temperature of 127 degrees, the

Sonoran Desert was among the hottest places in the United States. It was the home of the most ornery creatures in the West. Scorpions, tarantulas, and rattlesnakes combed the desert floor ready to sting, bite, and kill whatever got in their way. Coyotes, wolves, and hungry cougars preyed on rabbits or each other, whichever they could find to eat first. With its spiny body and beady black eyes, the grotesquely formed horned toad looked only slightly less ugly than the king of the desert lizards, the Gila monster, which everything avoided. At nearly two feet in length, with beadlike scales of orange, white, black, and brown, it was one of only two poisonous lizards in the world and the only one in the United States.

The vegetation in the Sonoran Desert also seemed designed

to keep humans out. The barrel cactus, prickly pear cactus, cholla cactus, and the giant saguaro cactus were armed with sharp needles that defied anyone to touch them. The saguaros stood more than forty feet tall, and some fifty, as if they were guarding all the creatures assigned to the place.

On the road to Gila Bend, Lionel and Barron slept in the wagon at night, unloading a portion of their canned goods to make a flat space for two. Although their travel day was cut short by temperatures in the nineties and hundreds, they made good time. By now they were in undershirts and trousers. Lionel was in stockings, finding his shoes too hot to bear. Starting at sunrise each day, they drove the mules for two hours at a stretch before taking a break for water and rest. They saw horned toads, tarantulas, and probably a Gila monster, which Barron described as "a huge lizard and snakelike animal with bright colors on its body." He knew enough not to touch it because of its "flicking tongue and bad appearance." More threatening to them were the relentless assaults on the mules and the wagon by armies of stinging ants. "They are everywhere," Barron said, "and we try to stop where there are none present, but if there is such a place we cannot find it!" The brothers were quick to reach Gila Bend in just eight days and nights, averaging nearly fifteen miles a day.

Following the wagon trail as it turned southeast at Gila Bend, Lionel and Barron began the most dangerous part of their journey. The road from Yuma to Gila Bend had been flat and the landscape nearly barren; the brothers could see whatever was moving toward them, including ants. The road from Gila Bend to Tucson became flanked by dense forests of prickly pear and saguaro cacti; Lionel and Barron couldn't tell what was five feet away from them on either side of the trail. Many of the predators in the Sonoran Desert lived in these cacti forests and fed at night.

It was along this stretch of the trail that the brothers saw the remains of draft animals and their masters who had misjudged the danger. "Bones of humans lay on either side of the road," Barron wrote, "marking the trail for travelers." Creeping through the cacti forest, the brothers encountered rattlesnakes nearly every day and occasionally a family of scorpions; they appeared in the middle of the road and stopped the mules dead in their tracks. Lionel and Barron drove the creatures away by kicking sand at them from a distance. Sometimes the brothers slept just a few hours a night. Sometimes they slept in shifts when the mules were spooked by howling coyotes or the sound of animals moving through the brush. The mules were everything and couldn't be lost. They were reminded of this, Barron noted, by the "vultures that circle in the air above us and follow us on the trail."

Averaging just under ten miles a day, they edged through the Sonoran Desert caked in sweat and sore on their backsides from sitting in the wagon for so long: This was the most frequent complaint Barron recorded after the blasting heat. During the final leg of the journey, they were relieved to meet some other people on the trail—the drivers and passengers of a Wells Fargo Overland Stage. Lionel and Barron encountered these stages two or three times a week when they zoomed past the wagon from either direction and buried the brothers in smothering dirt. Lionel called them "phantoms of the desert" in one of the few times he wrote in Barron's journal.

Started in 1858, the Wells Fargo Stage was horse-drawn and carried up to nine passengers and the United States mail along a

2,800-mile route from St. Louis, Missouri, to San Francisco, California, three days a week. To deliver the mail on time, the stage averaged 120 miles in twenty-four hours. There was little regard for passenger comfort. The drivers were called whips, and they had a standing order: "Remember, boys, nothing on God's earth must stop the United States mail." Few things did, as the whips roared along the Gila Trail, often half-drunk or completely drunk. One contemporary said the whips drank "more double-rectified, copper-distilled, trigger-lightning, sod-corn juice than a mountain man or an overland freighter."

One meeting occurred approximately eighty miles north of Tucson, when a stage driver stopped in the heat to change horses. Four trail horses were leashed to the back of the stage, and it took only a few minutes to hitch a fresh team. "We pulled alongside and asked one of the drivers for the distance to Tucson," Barron wrote. "He did not answer and was more set on changing the horses as fast as he could. He asked if we had seen any Indians and we said no." Six passengers were aboard, but they couldn't tell the brothers much about Tucson because they had spent only twenty minutes there for a meal of salt pork, coarse bread, and black coffee. They hadn't washed or slept in days and none had a clean face or clean teeth. Neither did Lionel and Barron. All they learned was that Tucson was a rest stop and not a destination for any of the passengers.

Eight days later the brothers reached the Santa Catalina Mountains just north of Tucson and saw the town below. But it was afternoon and too hot to travel the last seven miles. Perhaps it was also too depressing. The Catalinas were crawling with rattlesnakes and ants, and when the brothers made camp, the temperature was well over a hundred degrees; Tucson, a thousand feet below, would be hotter.

Looking down, Barron recorded, "The town is in the middle of a desert floor that extends for miles in each direction. There's a road leading into town and a river alongside. The landscape is of red sand and brush, but there is no sign of life anywhere except for some horses." He added, "The buildings have the shape of a rectangle, and I must say they appear to have been placed there by mistake." In fact, Tucson was located in the center of a giant frying pan, where the desert heat was trapped by surrounding

Giant saguaro cacti, photographed in the Sonoran Desert near Tucson around the time of Lionel and Barron's arrival.

mountains. People were living in the town, even if it wasn't apparent why.

But, happily, this was the last night of eating biscuits and beans and sleeping in the wagon surrounded by cacti. In the Santa Catalina Mountains at the last campsite, other plants yielded to the giant saguaro. To use Lionel's words, this was the last night of trying to sleep among "the silhouettes of these monsters in the darkness that surround us, the ghostly human-shaped figures whose only purpose in life seems to be to cause pain."

The modest Santa Cruz River ran alongside the trail that led from the mountains to Tucson and away from the cacti forest. Lionel and Barron started down the narrow strip the next morning, not with a song in their hearts but with sweat-stained shirts, dirt on their faces, sore rear ends, and relief at having reached their destination. It was the last week of July. After two months and eight days on the Gila Trail, they could only hope that Tucson was better up close than it appeared from a distance.

THREE

The Smell of Mesilla

The town that Lionel and Barron entered had the appearance of a place where no one would choose to live willingly. In this case looks weren't deceiving. "If we had known about the beauty of the place," Lionel wrote jokingly to his father, "we would have asked you to come with us." Tucson's appearance reflected its history of failure. It had been created from leftovers of Arizona's shaky history, and it was surprising that the town existed at all.

As a result of the war with Mexico, which ended in 1848, the United States acquired most of the Southwest, including part of Arizona north of the Gila River. Southern Arizona was considered worthless and not suited to be part of America. In arguing against annexing the region, the famous orator Senator Daniel Webster described it as "a barren waste of cactus and sand incapable of producing anything and therefore not worth keeping."

With the discovery of gold in California, migrants headed west on the Gila Trail through southern Arizona. They were easy prey for Apaches and Mexican bandits, who relieved travelers of their horses, wagons, and even the clothes they were wearing. To establish order in the area, the United States acquired southern Arizona in 1853 and built a series of forts along the Gila Trail to protect travelers: Fort McLane in New Mexico, Fort Yuma on

Tucson in the early 1870s. "A city of mud boxes, dingy and dilapidated, cracked and baked into a composite of dust and filth," wrote a visitor of the period.

the Colorado River, Fort Breckenridge north of Tucson, and Fort Buchanan south of Tucson.

The Spanish originally founded Tucson in the seventeenth century. After Apaches drove the Spanish out, Tucson was established for a second time in 1856, when four companies of soldiers were stationed on the east bank of the Santa Cruz River. They were eventually joined by drifters, disappointed gold seekers, thieves, murderers, and a few dozen prostitutes who, like the others, had no better place to go and no plans for doing anything worthwhile. Many had been kicked out of Texas and California or had fled from those places to avoid arrest.

As more misfits and malcontents arrived, Tucson acquired the reputation of being the first "Wild West" town. By 1860, five hundred Anglos, Native Americans, and Mexicans lived in Tucson. Most went about heavily armed. Shootings were so common that in 1860 the town's cemetery contained the graves of only two men who had died of natural causes. The population occupied itself with gambling, cockfights, and carousing, while the local garrison limited its activities to getting drunk. Meanwhile, Apaches threatened the town's existence again.

Before contact with the Spanish and Americans, approximately twelve thousand Apaches lived in Arizona and New Mexico. Led by Cochise and Geronimo, the Apaches fought whites who threatened to take their homeland and resented the establishment of white settlements, such as Tucson. With the outbreak of the American Civil War in 1861, the soldiers in the forts were withdrawn to fight in the East, and with no soldiers to check them, the Apaches went on the warpath. They regained control of southern Arizona and chased out many of the white settlers. Tucson's lawless inhabitants fled, and the town died— except for the rattlesnakes and scorpions living in its abandoned buildings.

The town began again in 1863, when Arizona was organized as a territory and the United States Army subdued the Apaches for a time. Led by the Indian fighter Kit Carson, the army killed 664 Apaches and captured 8,793 between 1863 and 1864. Attracted by rumors of gold in the mountains surrounding Tucson, some miners drifted into the town. A gold strike on the Gila River attracted 1,200 prospectors to the territory, and some of them followed the Santa Cruz River south to Tucson.

Throughout the 1850s, cowboys from Texas drove herds of cattle across Arizona to feed California's growing population.

Along the way they sold cattle to individuals who started ranches in the foothills and along the Santa Cruz River. During the same period, more than sixty thousand migrants passed through Tucson on their way to California, and some settled in southern Arizona and later in Tucson. Mexican-American cattlemen, ranchers, and miners moved in. Some Pimas and Hopis moved in to join the Papagos, who continued to worship at an old Spanish church near Tucson, even though it had no seats, no priest, and no other worshipers. The thieves, murderers, and prostitutes came back and in greater numbers, but in truth, southern Arizona was still a war zone. The Apaches whom Kit Carson hadn't killed had fled to Mexico, and they continued attacking travelers on the Gila Trail and white settlers in southern Arizona.

A Tucson street scene from the 1870s: rough adobe buildings and a muddy street without sidewalks.

Tucson: the view from the Palace Hotel.

By 1867, Tucson had a population of approximately thirteen hundred, and most of its residents lived in the town because it was the safest place in southern Arizona. Its future was still uncertain, and the only thing that was predictable about Tucson was heat and hostile Apaches.

Lionel and Barron approached Tucson from the north and parked their wagon on the outskirts of town. After washing and changing clothes, Barron left to scout the town on foot and locate space for the business. Lionel stayed with the merchandise, telling Barron to be quick in finding a place. The mules were exhausted, and it grew hotter by the hour. Lionel used the time to write their father, telling him that they had arrived safely and inquiring about family and friends. "Tucson," he observed, "looks like a ghost town with some horses and a few men wandering about. That's all there is to it."

Another visitor of the period gave a more extensive account. "Tucson," J. Ross Browne wrote in 1864, was "a city of mud boxes, dingy and dilapidated, cracked and baked into a composite of dust and filth; littered about with broken corrals, sheds, bake ovens, carcasses of dead animals, and broken pottery; barren of grass, parched, and grimly desolate in the glare of a scorching sun." On its streets were "sore-backed burros, coyote dogs, and naked children playing in the dirt; soldiers, teamsters, and miners soaked with fiery poison; and a noisy band of buffoons, cutting their antics to the most diabolical din of fiddles and guitars ever heard—these are what the traveler sees."

In surveying the town, Barron discovered there were already eight merchants competing for the limited market, the largest being Lord & Williams. Barron introduced himself to several merchants and inquired about rental space as he proceeded from one business to the next. Where there were sidewalks, they were wooden, but mostly there were no sidewalks. The dirt streets ran alongside the saloons, stables, hotels, eating establishments, and mescal shops. Most activity was centered in the saloons, but there was no shortage of customers wanting mescal beans; when chewed and ingested, they produced a powerful hallucinogenic state.

As Barron canvassed the town, packs of stray dogs fed on the garbage that was thrown into the streets. Along with the carcasses of dead animals, the streets were caked with deposits from horses, mules, dogs, and chickens, and the air had a distinctive smell. Flies buzzed from one pile to another. Ants crawled on the lumps. Rats scurried from under the sidewalks for a taste. It was into this world that Barron stepped, wearing boots like most everyone in Tucson.

Having learned what he could in a few hours, he returned to the wagon, and the brothers drove it to a livery stable down Main Street, weaving through the garbage and the remains of dead animals. As they proceeded, the merchants Barron had previously met greeted the brothers with the wave of a hand. Others just stared—Pimas, Papagos, Mexicans, Mexican-Americans, and Anglos, some of whom were slumped over on benches in front of the saloons and mescal shops. Lionel's impression of the town up close was reported by his brother in a brief entry: "Lionel thinks sanitation is the town's chief distinction, or rather lack of it. He says that you, Pa, should have the fortune of being with us so you could enjoy the smell. He is joking, of course."

The brothers made friends with Charles Etchells, who owned a livery stable and wagon shop. After boarding the mules and wagon, they spent the rest of the day visiting businesses and making acquaintances. The first decision the brothers made on their own was to be bold, not timid, in trying to succeed as frontier merchants. Instead of distancing themselves from the competition, they rented an empty store next to Lord & Williams, the largest and most successful mercantile firm in Tucson.

Lord & Williams's store on Mesilla Street.

Located at the corner of Main and Mesilla streets, the store had the advantage of being downtown in what downtown there was. There were other shops along Mesilla to draw customers to the area: a tailor shop, a restaurant, and Foster's Saloon. Mesilla had sidewalks, a sure sign of distinction—although few streets could top its odor, because it intersected with heavily caked Main Street. "Lionel paid sixty-five dollars for the first month's rent," Barron wrote, "and the owner, Mr. Leopold Carrillo, was glad to have the money. His wife gave us a dinner of fried beans, tortillas, and water, and we were glad to have it."

The brothers passed their first night in Tucson in the Phillips House, one of only two hotels in town. "We spent some pleasant hours," Barron said, "playing cards with the other boarders, a wagon driver and two men from Texas in cattle raising." Barron related how Lionel had the Texans "laughing wildly" as he whirled about, mimicking their efforts to brush the stinging ants off their clothing and faces. He also noted that the brothers drank more than a few glasses of bourbon "to wash away the trail dust and celebrate the end of our ordeal."

They spent the next day unloading the contents of their wagon into the store. Like the other spaces for rent, their store had bare adobe walls, a dirt floor, and nothing inside. By mid-afternoon it had turned into an oven, but the brothers worked through the heat building makeshift tables and shelves out of planks and scrap boards. They stacked the cans in rows so that the labels and hand-written descriptions could be seen: BEANS, STEW, CHILI, MEAT. Cans that had lost their labels and whose contents were unknown were placed on a separate table with dented or smashed cans. Lionel made a sign to hang outside announcing the opening of the Mark Jacobs Company. But before he nailed the sign in place, the brothers prepared to meet their customers. Tucson was about to see what it was getting in the Jacobs brothers, Lionel and Barron.

They washed, shaved, and put on fresh shirts and clean trousers with suspenders. They cleaned their boots and put on a coat of polish to cover the lingering odor from Tucson's filthy streets. They gave the appearance of gentlemen who chose to live in Tucson and who believed in its future, and their clothing, man-ners, and education set them apart from most others in town. With neatly combed hair and pride in who he was, Lionel stood on the sidewalk in front of the store greeting shoppers and announcing the business. Appearing much the same, Barron greeted customers as they entered the store and left with a can of this and a can of that. In San Francisco, the stock was purchased for twelve to twenty-five cents per can; in Tucson, each can was priced at a dollar, and the brothers sold out in just under a week.

It did not matter that Lord & Williams next door sold more goods in a day than Lionel and Barron did in a week. It did not matter that their sleeping quarters in a small room off the back of the store were cramped and uncomfortable. The heat didn't matter. The smell of Mesilla didn't matter. "We end the first week a success in the business," Barron wrote to his father. "We can now call ourselves frontier merchants. We made the trip and sold the goods, and the future holds great promise." They had made the trip and sold the goods, and none of the town's vulgarities had dragged them down.

FOUR

Stern-Wheelers, Four-Inchers, and the Nigh

Having succeeded in their first week in Tucson, Lionel and Barron were optimistic about the future. They sold the canned goods at a profit, as planned. They sold the wagon and mules at a profit, as planned. Conveying the happy news, Lionel wrote, "Mr. Etchells paid us twelve hundred dollars, for a profit of four hundred dollars, and we are relieved never to sit in that buckboard again." As planned, Lionel and Barron mailed the profits from the canned goods and the wagon, which Mark used to buy more merchandise. In addition, they had a plan for solving the problem of transportation, which all frontier merchants faced. On paper it looked like a good idea.

There were three ways of transporting merchandise to Tucson, and Mark considered each one. Some merchants shipped goods by railroad from New York to Independence, Missouri, where the merchandise was loaded in freight wagons and hauled along the Santa Fe Trail through Kansas, Oklahoma, and New Mexico to Tucson. It was a safe route through populated areas, but it was the longest route at nearly three thousand miles. Transportation costs and the five months it took to get merchandise from New York to Arizona drove up the price of goods and made competition difficult. Mark said no.

Other merchants shipped goods on ocean steamers from San Francisco to the port of Guaymas in the Gulf of California. From there the cargo went by freight wagons through the Mexican province of Sonora to Tucson. At just under four hundred miles, it was a short trip from Guaymas to Tucson, and the entire trade route of eight hundred miles from San Francisco took only two and a half months. But Mexican bandits in Sonora made this route hazardous, and customs officials at Guaymas made it expensive; sometimes they charged two fees for importing goods—one for the government and one for themselves. Mark said no.

The third route was by ocean steamer from San Francisco to the mouth of the Colorado River in the Gulf of California, then by river steamboats to Yuma, and, finally, by freight wagons on the Gila Trail to Tucson—a trip of approximately three months. Mark decided on the Colorado River route, writing to Barron that it was "comparatively inexpensive and safe." Lionel responded: "'Safe' isn't the word I would use to describe the road from Yuma to Tucson. Still, we trust your judgment. We've heard of problems on the river when the water is too low for navigation." Mark had heard that also, but other merchants used the route, and he stuck to his choice.

Using his store in San Bernardino as collateral, Mark had borrowed six thousand dollars to get the business started. The first shipment of goods was already on its way when the brothers left San Diego for Tucson. It was a typical load weighing twenty-five hundred pounds and valued at three thousand dollars in San Francisco. "It arrived in fine shape," Barron wrote, two weeks after the brothers had sold the last of their canned goods. Before it arrived, they used their spare time to make improvements in the store. They built permanent shelving, laid a floor of wooden planks, bought some chairs and a desk, and hired a carpenter to build a 20-by-3-foot counter with a surface of polished oak.

After the first shipment arrived, they went back to the business of selling. Happily, they sold most of the cargo within three months, before the second load rolled into town "in fine shape," Barron reported again. Happily, they sold most of it by the time the third shipment rolled in. But two months later, in June 1868, the fourth shipment was sitting on the bottom of the Colorado River. "Our transportation plan needs more work," Lionel wrote with some sarcasm.

When the boat carrying the goods rammed a log in a sandbar, Lionel and Barron experienced the reality of frontier merchandising: It wasn't as easy as they thought, in spite of their early success. When the boat sank, the Tucson store was still in debt. Mark was counting on profits from the fourth shipment to pay for the merchandise, which he had purchased on credit. Because of one worthless log stuck in the sand, Mark was forced to declare bankruptcy. Lionel and Barron were forced to close their store.

The brothers could communicate with their father every eight days, if the mail stage between Arizona and California wasn't robbed by bandits or attacked by Apaches. So the brothers wrote every eight days, with Barron doing most of the corresponding, and the focus of the letters was transportation. While they discussed a new strategy, Lionel took a job as a cowboy at a ranch, herding cattle from one grazing area to another. He enjoyed wearing the buckskin hat and chaps and the horse riding. Barron took a part-time job baling hay on a farm but said nothing about the work. They still slept in the small room at the back of the store, which was now empty.

After a month of haggling with creditors, Mark devised a bankruptcy settlement and cleared his debts. A week later, in July 1868, he transferred control of the San Bernardino store to a business partner, moved the family to San Francisco, and invested three thousand dollars in another shipment to Tucson, the fifth. Having lost his credit, Mark had to pay for all of his purchases in cash this time. As the shipment left San Francisco, Mark wrote, "I trust we have solved our problems and will succeed without further difficulties." He and his sons could only hope that they had made the right changes in shipping goods to Tucson: Transportation was the cornerstone of their business.

Previously Mark had hired several forwarding agents to arrange for transportation from the Gulf of California to Tucson. One inspected the goods at the mouth of the Colorado River and loaded the cargo on shore. Another signed a contract with the Colorado Steam Navigation Company to carry the goods 130 miles upriver to Yuma. A third received the merchandise at Yuma and made arrangements for freighting to Tucson. Mark's system of using several forwarding agents had worked until one of them hired the wrong steamboat captain and the fourth shipment was lost.

After pondering the situation, Lionel came up with the idea of hiring one agent to oversee all transportation between the Gulf of California and Tucson. "We need one person," Lionel declared to Mark, "one man we can count on for this part of the business." On his own initiative, Lionel took time off from his job as a cowboy and boarded a stage for Yuma. He spent three days there interviewing forwarding agents before hiring one. His name was David Neahr, and in the summer of 1868 he replaced the patchwork of agents previously used. "Neahr has a reputation for efficiency," Lionel informed Mark, "and I trust him."

Starting with the fifth shipment in July 1868, all cargo labeled MARK JACOBS COMPANY, TUCSON was assigned to DAVID NEAHR, YUMA. Every two weeks or so Barron wrote to Mark specifying the items, and every three months Mark checked the schedule of the next steamer bound for the Gulf of California: the *Centennial, Newborn, Montana, Laura,* or *Clara Bell.* He made the purchases a few days before the vessel departed, and after the cargo was weighed and loaded he paid the entire bill for shipping, as required by the boat's captain. The price averaged fourteen cents a pound, but it fluctuated up and down, and a typical ship-

The double-deck steamer *Gila* on the Colorado River.

ment of twenty-five hundred pounds could easily cost four hundred dollars.

Neahr's men received the goods in the Gulf, contracted with a boat captain they knew personally, and Neahr handled the rest once the boat reached Yuma. For his services, Neahr charged four cents a pound, more than many forwarding agents in Yuma. But he had never lost a shipment, except for one boat that had moored near a camp of Apache warriors.

Neahr knew all the boat captains and who could be trusted to navigate the tricky Colorado with its ever-shifting sandbars. They sailed on one of the double-deck steamers owned by the Colorado Steam Navigation Company: the *Gila, Uncle Sam, General Jessup, Esmeralda,* or *Cocopah.* The boats were unusually wide so they could carry heavy loads in shallow water. The captains were called pilots, and sometimes they had to navigate in less than two feet of water. Experienced pilots preferred the stern-wheelers to the side-wheelers for better steering around the sandbars, and these men knew how to beat the river in places where it was only a foot deep: They reversed the boat, backed the stern-wheel into the shallow water, and used the paddle wheel literally to chew a path through the sand and muck.

As a shipment neared Yuma, Neahr wrote to Tucson, usually to Lionel, discussing river traffic and when the cargo would probably arrive. They discussed flooding along the Gila Trail, the fluctuating prices for freighting between Yuma and Tucson, and Apaches, if recent events deemed it necessary. At Yuma, the entire investment was turned over to a rough-looking man in a cowboy hat and his partner, the "swamper," who carried a rifle. The freighters charged an average of fourteen cents a pound, which

The building that housed David Neahr's business in Yuma, photographed in ruins in the late 1880s.

added another three hundred fifty dollars to transportation costs. But having made the trip themselves in a wagon, Lionel and Barron knew the freighters earned their pay. For a typical shipment, the total cost of transportation plus Neahr's fee averaged close to a thousand dollars.

From a distance of five miles, an onlooker could tell when a team left Yuma for the three-week haul to Tucson: The horizon became cloudy with a rising trail of dust. The freighters were called mule skinners and they had an extensive knowledge of weather, geography, and Apaches, which allowed them to operate where few dared to go. Perhaps one of every five hundred skinners was killed by Apaches, which had something to do with their reputation for drinking, swearing, and barroom brawling.

The skinners used huge Carson wagons. Frequently a team of

twenty-four mules was used to pull three wagons that were care-fully loaded to distribute weight for making sharp turns. The lead wagon was called a four-inch wagon. Its eight-foot-high wheels were four inches wide. It carried 6,500 pounds. The "swing" or center wagon was a three-and-a-half-inch wagon and carried 5,500 pounds. The trail wagon was a three-incher and took a load of 4,500 pounds. Standard accessories included water kegs, feed for the mules, extra ammunition, and whiskey.

Like the river pilots, the mule skinners were specialists in their craft, but they were only as good as their mules. They knew more about mules than anyone in the West, and they knew mules to be superior to other draft animals. Of the three kinds of draft ani-mals used in the West—the horse, mule, and ox—the mule had the longest average working life, about eighteen years. Some worked as long as thirty years. At twelve years of age, a mule was just attaining its full strength, whereas a horse of the same age was beginning to decline. Mules could do as much work as a horse on one-third less food, were subject to fewer diseases, and had tough hides that made them resistant to harness sores. They must have traveled a million miles lugging freight to Billings, Montana; Boise, Idaho; Cheyenne, Wyoming; Denver, Colorado; Salt Lake City, Utah; Albuquerque, New Mexico; and Tucson, Arizona. And they were intelligent in their work.

When a team pulled out of Yuma—stretching nearly a hundred feet in length—only a mule skinner could appreciate the beauty of each animal or understand its position in the team. A pair of mules was called a span, and the skinner selected the two largest mules for the "wheelers." The span of wheelers was positioned directly in front of the wagon—the only mules connected to the wagon tongue. Because of their strength, the wheelers had the best traction for pulling up steep grades and holding back on downgrades.

The most nimble and knowledgeable span was selected as the leaders, and the most intelligent of these two was always positioned on the left. He was called the nigh, and he gave direction to the whole team. Only the leaders and the wheelers were fitted with bridles and bits, and the driver gave orders to the nigh through a single rein attached to the left side of the nigh's bit. A long, steady pull swung the nigh to the left. A series of sharp jerks caused him to throw his head up and to the right to avoid the pain of the bit, causing the team to turn right. On sharp turns the nigh and his mate often had to leave the trail to swing wide and scramble over rocks and brush so the rest could stay on the trail. The other spans were matched for similar size and strength and were positioned according to their willingness to take orders from the nigh. Except for the wheelers, the more intelligent the mule, the closer he was to the nigh.

When a freight train rolled into Tucson carrying merchandise from San Francisco, it was the result of careful planning, hard work, and luck. It was also costly, and when the fifth shipment of goods reached Lionel and Barron in September 1868, they wasted no time unloading the merchandise from the wagons. By then they had made further improvements in the store. The counter was in place with shelves underneath for receipts and correspondence. They had more shelf space and tables, and within a day most empty spaces were filled with the newly arrived items.

The shipment signified that their father still had faith in the business, and on September 8, Mark wrote a letter of encouragement to his sons, saying, "We will have the opportunity of suc-ceeding with each one of us doing our part. I trust your friend David Neahr will not let us down."

"It was nice to have received your letter," Lionel wrote back, "and nice to see merchandise in the store again, thanks to Mr. Neahr. Put your faith in Barron's and my judgment. After occu-pying ourselves with other jobs for the past two months, we are glad to be occupied with business again, thanks to Mr. Neahr." Lionel had solved the transportation problem, and he wasn't going to let his father forget it.

FIVE

The Shoo Fly Feeling

By the time Lionel solved the transportation problem, the military headquarters and territorial capital had been moved to Tucson. This was the reason the brothers had come to the frontier town in the first place, although the changes in Tucson weren't apparent right away. Barron said, "We see more soldiers and more men wearing suits, but that is the extent of our new status." Lionel wrote that it would take some time for Tucson to have "the appearance of being the capital of the territory." It was easy to see why in the summer of 1868.

The governor didn't have a governor's house and the new capital didn't have its own building. Officials conducted business in rooms with dirt floors and mud roofs near the downtown district, and members of the legislature met in Foster's Saloon—that is, if they could get to Tucson. Andrew Gibbons and Octavious Glass made the trip in September 1868, after being elected to the legislature from towns in the remote northwestern corner of the territory. They described their ride down the Colorado River in a fourteen-foot boat as "terrifying." And when they reached Yuma, they discovered that all stage service to Tucson had been canceled after an Apache attack took the lives of all eight passengers and the drivers of a Wells Fargo stage. The lawmakers arrived six days late and missed the governor's speech about the main problem for settlers in the territory: Apaches.

During the summer of 1868, travelers still spent the night on a "Tucson bed"—an armful of straw tossed in the corner of a corral. Mule-drawn carts hauled barrels of springwater to town, where the water was sold for five cents a bucket, and peddlers still got twenty-five cents each for empty tin cans that people used as drinking cups. At night oil lamps and rags dipped in saucers of grease provided the town's only light, and the saloons were packed with unbathed men breathing whiskey fumes and swirling clouds of tobacco smoke.

Most of the news in the town concerned the relocation of the capital, but for two weeks in September residents were deprived of their issues of *The Arizonian* newspaper because the editor went camping. The streets hadn't changed. John Bourke, a newly arrived soldier, jokingly reported on how locals gave directions to strangers: "You want to find the governor's? Wa'al, podner, jest keep right down this yer street past the Palace S'loon, till yer gets to the second manure pile on yer right, then keep to yer left pas' the post office, 'n' yer'll see a dead burro in the middle of th' road . . . 'n' jes' beyond, that's the gov's outfit. Can't miss it."

The appearance of Tucson hadn't changed, but its economy had. With the arrival of the military and the government, the town's population increased from thirteen hundred to more than three thousand. Twice a year the Army paymaster came to pay the eight hundred soldiers stationed outside of town, and they spent their money on a variety of merchandise and on whiskey and prostitutes. Far more important were the Mexican-American farmers and ranchers who supplied the military with hay, wood,

Neighbors and competitors in Tucson's growing economy: the Zeckendorf and Roca businesses, photographed about 1880.

flour, and beef. When these suppliers came to town, they had a lot of money to spend, and they needed all kinds of goods. "They're the prime customers," Barron wrote. "Our success depends upon them."

To secure the new customers, Lionel spent most evenings in Tucson's saloons, sometimes accompanied by Barron. Outgoing and free in sharing his bottle with others, Lionel was quick to learn the Mexican dialect and quick to make friends. As a conversation proceeded, he noted that a farmer needed baling wire or a rancher needed a certain medicine to cure his cattle of a disease. His standard reply was, "I can get it in three months." He became known as a man of his word and as a merchant who could acquire specialty items: a banjo, a butterfly net, an artificial limb. He also acquired a reputation for being able to hold his own in a fight, usually as the result of trying to break up an existing brawl. In casual references to such activity, Barron wrote, "Lionel was not much hurt" and "Lionel interceded with others" and "Lionel said the man was too drunk to swing with any authority."

Although Lionel may have brought in most of the early customers, his friends became Barron's friends once they entered the store to pick up their specialty items—and it was Barron who actually placed the orders. This was an important part of the business, and as Barron said, "I take it upon myself as the most suitable person for it." His standard orders consisted of manufactured items that were scarce on the frontier: canned goods, cloth, boots, hats, shoes, belts, glassware, and eating utensils. But an order might also include a loom, a case of expensive wine, a fishbowl, a music box, and once "a dozen boomerangs." Each specialty item was an indication that the brothers knew their customers personally, and Barron took care in describing the specialty items so there would be no mistake—for example, "sheet music for flute and violin duo" and "one birdcage of medium height suitable for two occupants."

Two thirds of the town's population was Hispanic, and it was Barron who learned how to conduct business with his and Lionel's Mexican-American customers. When a farmer or rancher announced that he was going to town, his neighbors usually gave him seven to ten Mexican dollars and a list of needed items. The first thing he did on entering the store was to take off his wide leather belt, which had a partition in the center and contained "from one hundred fifty to two hundred dollars," Barron reported. Laying the belt on the oak counter, the customer started to buy the articles on his first list while Lionel or Barron counted the amount inside the belt. As the customer gathered each item and placed it on the counter, whoever was minding the counter recorded the amount of the purchase. Usually it was Barron.

The accounting method the brothers used was explained to Mark in a letter Barron wrote entitled "How We Do Business." It started with a horizontal line on a sheet of paper and ended with a series of marks on the paper that looked like some bewildering code. The Mexican dollar was divided into fifty cents, twenty-five cents, and twelve and a half cents. A short mark above the line meant twelve and half cents; a line drawn above and below the center line meant twenty-five cents. A half circle above the line meant fifty cents; an entire circle through the line meant a dollar. A V above the line meant five dollars; and an X on the horizontal line meant ten dollars. It wasn't anything like the accounting method Mark had taught his sons, but Tucson was Tucson and business was good.

Lionel and Barron sold most everything they ordered, including Lionel's specialty items. They paid six and a half cents for a bar of soap in San Francisco and sold it for twenty-five cents in Tucson. Coffee cost sixty cents a pound and sold for two dollars. Sugar cost eighty-five cents a pound and sold for three dollars. A barrel of flour cost five dollars and sold for twenty-five dollars. Like the other firms, they lost shipments to Apaches and bandits, and their store was often damaged by summer floods, which eroded the outside walls. They repaired the walls, continued ordering and selling, and their hard work paid off. Between 1867 and 1869, four merchants in Tucson declared bankruptcy and went out of business. Lionel and Barron didn't. By 1869, they had paid off the original investment in the business and were showing a profit. "It seems we have done most things right," Barron reported, "and have a good share of the business."

After Mark's loan was paid off in June 1869, Lionel and Barron got to keep 40 percent of the profits. For a time they put most of their money back into the store. A hardwood floor and paneling on the walls and ceiling gave the store a finished look and helped keep it clean. A cash register, a safe, and hooks on one wall for hanging hats made the place look businesslike and sociable.

It wasn't luck that made the Mark Jacobs Company of Tucson profitable. It was Lionel and Barron. Before their business showed a profit, they joined the community of Tucson, in its saloons and elsewhere, and staked their future lives on the success of the town. They might have cursed Tucson for its crudeness, but they didn't. They might have remained distant and aloof, but they didn't. They had more education and better manners than most of the town's residents, but they didn't show it in a way that was disrespectful. They made friends with anyone who would be their friend and embraced them not just as customers but also as members of a community on its way to becoming something better. Successful merchants were community builders, and they knew most everyone.

Lionel and Barron knew Samuel Bostwick, the first African-American businessman in Tucson. He opened a barbershop in 1869, and the brothers patronized it. Lionel also said that Samuel was "the best fiddle player in town." They knew Alexander Levin, a fat, jolly, outgoing German, who started the Pioneer Brewery and Dance Hall and bought the Hodges Hotel in 1869. That year Lionel and Barron moved out of their room in the store and became tenants in the hotel. Joey Peel, a nephew of Samuel Bostwick, moved into the spare room in the store and served as a night watchman and stock man and general helper during the day.

Lionel and Barron knew Charlie Dumas, a Frenchman who opened a drugstore in 1868 and became so skillful at preparing drugs that he was called "Doctor" Dumas. They knew Mrs. William Osborn. She purchased cloth in the brothers' store to sew curtains, which made her crude adobe home more livable. Her husband was probate judge, a U.S. marshal, and one of Lionel's close friends. Mrs. Josephine Hughes from Pennsylvania was an acquaintance of Barron's. She purchased a flock of chickens to get rid of the tarantulas and scorpions darting across the mud floors of her house, then laid a wooden floor and covered it with carpet ordered by Barron. Nearly everyone knew "Seven-Toed Pete," including Barron, who was fond of gambling. During most evenings Barron could be found at the Fashion Saloon, where Pete dealt cards wearing his specially made shoes. Barron did not wager a great deal of money and considered the night a success if he broke even.

While establishing friendships, Lionel and Barron joined the routine of frontier life. During the week, it was conducting business in the store and doing everyday things such as squashing tarantulas and scorpions that had wandered in, scraping off deposits that had been tracked in from the street, and occasionally getting into a fistfight with a customer who had been caught stealing but wouldn't own up to it. Lionel did most of the fighting and considered it "part of doing business." He also seemed to enjoy it, which made him fit into the town perfectly. And there was the routine of the heat, which meant conducting business in clothing drenched in sweat.

Normally on Sunday mornings, the brothers walked to a shower house on the west side of town, where men gathered for socializing and washing at ten cents a customer. A real bath in a tin washtub, Barron explained, was "too expensive at a dollar a customer." But he added, "Travelers gladly pay seventy-five cents to have their hair washed in a horse trough behind the Cosmopolitan Hotel."

After showering, the brothers made wagers on cockfights, horse races, and foot races, where Lionel was a contender and sometimes won. If there was a fiesta, they bought tortillas and carne seca from vendors while they walked down Main Street enjoying the music but watching where they stepped. On Saturdays they

The Congress Hall Saloon, one of the places where Lionel and Barron kept up acquaintances with their customers.

met at the home of William Zeckendorf or Philip Drachman for worship with the town's other Jewish residents, who numbered less than fifty. The brothers said little about keeping the Jewish faith except that they did so on Saturday and looked forward to "devotion and socializing."

At the close of each business day, they took a meal in one of Tucson's restaurants. Sometimes they ate at the Hodges Hotel, the Congress Hall Saloon, or the Cosmopolitan. Sometimes they went to Maisson d'Or, Won Tai's Celestial Restaurant, or the Poodle Dog Café. But at the close of a typical business day, they headed for the Shoo Fly Café.

Mrs. Florence Wallen owned the Shoo Fly and gave her restaurant the name because, she said, "The flies won't shoo worth a cent." Opened in 1868, it wasn't much more than a long, narrow adobe room with a low ceiling and yellow walls. Mrs. Wallen required that all meals be paid for in advance. Regular patrons received napkins, but otherwise they received no special treatment. Customers sat at rickety pine tables and were served by two Mexican boys attired in baggy trousers and white jackets with colorful red sashes. There was no menu because every meal was the same: bacon, chicken, or jerked beef that was made into a stew. To distinguish her business from other eating establishments, or to demonstrate her sense of humor—Barron wasn't sure which—Mrs. Wallen hung a pair of dried jackrabbit ears on the wall.

Although service was slow and some customers grumbled about the flies, the place was usually crowded by seven P.M. Most patrons saw the flies as an indication that the food was edible, and customers were allowed to stay at the tables for hours after eating, "it being the inclination of the owner to prepare enough food for about two hours," Barron observed. The brothers were usually eating by seven o'clock, and by eight they were leaning back in their chairs, puffing cigars and talking to their friends. Their friends also ate at the Cosmopolitan and the Poodle Dog, but the Shoo Fly felt like home.

SIX

Fifty Cigars and Perfumy

In the 1870s, Tucson became important as a center for trade and transportation and its economy grew at a steady pace. Starting in 1870, Lionel and Barron used their profits from the store to invest in other businesses. Their goal was to make extra money and also strengthen the economy of southern Arizona, which would help ensure the continued success of their store. Although they acted together and were cautious before making a move, they made mistakes, and it was left to Barron to report the bad news to Mark.

"Dear Pa," Barron wrote in June 1870. "We were forced to sell the freight wagons, with which we had hoped to capture some of the freighting business between Yuma and Tucson. We paid $5,500 and sold them for $4,000." "Dear Pa," Barron wrote in August 1870. "Our investment in the buckboards has failed. We had planned to win the mail contract from Tucson to New Mexico, but our bid was not accepted." After Mexican cattle rustlers caused an investment in Mexican cattle to backfire, Mark wrote to Barron, "Stick to the business in Tucson. There is nothing like it." Whether this was an order or just advice isn't clear, but it prompted a rare letter from Lionel that was eight pages long.

Dated September 5, 1870, it said, "Barron and I have invested in the Star Flouring Mill in the eastern part of the territory, and we are making money." True. "It was only because of the power of Wells Fargo Freighting…that we failed in previous enterprises." Probably true. "If we haven't made a great deal of money, we haven't lost a great deal either, but there is something else. We've earned the trust that you deny us, and neither of us deserves being called 'foolish.' Pa, it is our money to use as we see fit." In a departure from his customary signature "Lionel," he closed, "Your loving sons, Barron and Lionel."

Thereafter, Mark said little about his sons' investments. The investments continued and increased, marking a turning point in the brothers' lives. Lionel was like a man banging on a door to get at the money on the other side and also win his father's respect. Barron was more like a man pushing against the door—but for the same reasons. They learned from their early mistakes, and their close relationship helped give them the confidence they needed to succeed in other business ventures.

Their first break came in October 1870, when they won a government contract to transport flour from the Star Flouring Mill to Fort Breckenridge and Fort Buchanan. The prominent rancher and part-owner of the mill, Henry Hooker, helped the brothers win the contract, which provided a long-term source of income. A year later, in 1871, they captured the beef contracts for the forts, thanks to Lionel's friend and bar mate, the cattleman Hector Sanchez. Increasingly Lionel spent less time in the saloons and Barron fewer hours gambling. Their lives were changing along with the West.

With each order for merchandise, Barron conveyed the good

news. They made money by investing in cattle again, selling beef to the government, and shipping the hides to California for manufacture into leather. They made money by shipping merchandise to Mexico after rich ore deposits were discovered along the San Miguel River near Ures. Goods in Ures sold for three times what they did in Tucson. To profit from the soldier trade, in July 1872 they opened a branch store near Camp Lowell, seven miles northeast of Tucson. To profit from Tucson's increasing demand for merchandise, in September 1872 they bought out a rival merchant, a Mr. A. Lazard, and relocated to a larger store on Main Street, four stores down from Lord & Williams, still the biggest firm in town.

As they had done before, the brothers invested part of their profits in the new store. Now their shipments of merchandise averaged 12,000 pounds, not 2,500, and Lionel and Barron had enough reserve cash to survive practically any calamity and enough to invest in new money-making schemes. Reversing his earlier position, Mark wrote, "Keep up your good work. Invest no more than 20 percent of profits in any enterprise, unless Lionel thinks otherwise and you agree." This must have pleased Lionel, but he felt no need to show it.

While they continued to accumulate wealth, Lionel and Barron were drawn into civic affairs. Their store was a center for socializing, just as the Shoo Fly was, and at any time during business hours there might be a dozen men standing in groups and talking. Dressed in tailored suits and clean boots, some of the men sat on the city council and asked the brothers for advice on policy. One thing led to another and on January 3, 1871, Lionel was appointed to the Pima County Board of Supervisors; within a week he was elected chairman. Barron told Mark, "Lionel takes the office as a matter of duty, but he seems to enjoy it also." Later that year a mass meeting was held downtown and Lionel was recommended for a seat in the legislature. Lionel wrote Mark, "It should not take away from business, and I will see that it won't." Without campaigning and running unopposed, he won the election and served in the legislature. There he was forced to confront what had always been the number-one problem for settlers in the territory.

There were two opinions on what should be done about the warring Apaches. It was the policy of the United States government to negotiate peace with the Apaches and let them live on the San Carlos Indian Reservation northeast of Tucson or at one of the camps in southern Arizona maintained for that purpose. After years of warfare with the Great Plains tribes—the Sioux, Cheyenne, Comanche, and Arapaho—public opinion in the East favored peace, with war only as a last resort to protect settlers.

The second opinion was reflected in the attitude of the Indian fighter Kit Carson. Referring to Apaches, Kit Carson said, "All Indian men of that tribe are to be killed whenever and wherever you can find them." This was also the view of most whites in the territory and in the legislature. It was practically unthinkable for a white person to defend Apaches, and the main business of the legislature was to urge the government to send more soldiers and conduct more campaigns until all the Apaches were dead.

At the time Lionel assumed office, residents were screaming for revenge because of recent Apache attacks. Although some farmers and ranchers had been killed by Apaches, residents were most outraged over the case of Larcena Pennington, a young woman who had been traveling outside of Tucson and was captured by

Apaches. She was beaten, raped, stripped of her clothing, and left for dead. Miraculously, she survived. In spite of a broken leg and a battered body, she crawled back to Tucson, living for days on roots and berries.

Residents got their revenge in a massacre at Camp Grant, sixty miles northeast of Tucson. On April 30, 1871, a force of 148 men, a mixture of Anglos, Mexican-Americans, and Papagos, attacked a band of Apaches at Camp Grant and killed more than a hundred women and children. Only eight of the dead were men; the others were away hunting. Shocked at the crime and reports of mutilation and rape, residents in the East demanded that the murderers be brought to trial. They were, and a Tucson jury acquitted them all. Support for the acquittal was widespread

Participants in the Camp Grant massacre murder trial outside the Pima County Courthouse in Tucson, December 1871.

in the territory and in the legislature, whose members continued to call for the complete elimination of the Apaches.

Lionel wasn't among them. The only references he or Barron made to Apaches were neutral observations, as if they were uncertain of their beliefs or perhaps thought it best not to express them. They would say, "John Dawson was killed by Apaches and his wagon and animals taken" and "Apaches have stopped all freighting through Sonora." In the midst of the screaming for Apache blood, Lionel never joined the cry to kill Apaches and said nothing about the verdict of acquittal for the Camp Grant murders. His friends in the legislature must have wondered about his silence and what he carried in his heart. He never did say.

Following his term in the legislature, Lionel served on committees for sanitation and schools and helped establish the Tucson Mercantile Association in 1875. He was Territorial Treasurer and sat on the Tucson City Council. Barron later held the same offices, although Barron never served in the legislature. The brothers were leaders in passing laws prohibiting the dumping of garbage within the city limits and prohibiting the butchering of animals on the city's streets.

As their business activities expanded in 1873 and 1874, Lionel and Barron were joined by relatives. Their nephew Abraham Franklin managed much of the brothers' out-of-town business. He was only eighteen when he wrote about buying cattle in Mexico and dealing with the outlaw John Ringo. Ringo and his band of rustlers would stampede herds in Abraham's care, then Abraham would have to hire Ringo to round up the "strays" for a sum of one hundred dollars. Later Abraham ran a branch store in Safford, Arizona, northeast of Tucson, along with Albert Jacobs, Lionel and Barron's seventeen-year-old brother.

Starting in 1875, other relatives were brought in to manage the Tucson store while Lionel and Barron took turns traveling on buying trips and overseeing their other investments in southern Arizona. At the time, Lionel was thirty-five and Barron was twenty-nine. Every three months or so, one of them traveled to San Francisco for on-site purchases and to visit family and friends. They also made trips to New York, where they established their own line of credit for investments. Dressed in neatly tailored suits and hats that were in fashion, they gave the appearance of wealth and position, and if either happened to meet a nice young Jewish woman, the trip was made that much more pleasant. Their circle of friends outside of Tucson contained several candidates for marriage. It wasn't clear if Barron was looking for a wife, but it was clear that his older brother wasn't.

It wasn't because Lionel was shy in romance. If anything, he was excessive. Since they shared most everything, Barron probably knew the approximate number of girlfriends his brother had in New York and San Francisco, but it wasn't reported in any letter to Mark. When Lionel was in Tucson, his girlfriends wrote to him, and although he wasn't counting, the women who loved him numbered at least two dozen. One of them named Mimmie, and like the others, she was captivated by Lionel. "Dearest Lionel," Mimmie wrote in one letter, "I wish you could fly to me this moment. I've such a sweet little kiss for you & I'm going to keep it till you come. . . . Oh darling, even now I see your sweet face, so smiling and full of love for me, but I confess that I begun to love you too dearly, for truly I could not bear to think of you with someone else. . . . Please when you retire tonight, imagine Mim stooping at your bedside imprinting a thousand kisses on your lips and oh such a tight embrace. . . . I shall try to prove myself worthy of your affections."

Some women wrote to Barron when he was in Tucson, but their letters were nothing like Mim's. Barron kept a personal memo book with neatly marked entries, such as "$70 for charity" and "$100 for the school fund." And then there was an entry every two weeks or so that was always the same: "50 cigars and perfumy." In a world of ever more complicated business transactions, it was possible to smoke fifty cigars in two weeks at an average of four a day. It was possible to exhaust a full bottle of perfume in two weeks, had Barron been known to wear perfume, which he wasn't. These entries in his memo book were reminders to himself that he had purchased fifty cigars and had visited the section of Tucson known as the Wedge.

The Calle de la India Triste—Street of the Sad Indian Girl—was the old Spanish name for a three-block-long street that ran parallel to Congress Street, which ran from downtown to the outskirts of town. Over the years businesses encroached on the Calle de la India Triste and pushed it toward Congress until the two streets eventually intersected near downtown. The three-block area in between had the shape of a piece of pie and was called the Wedge. When Barron visited there, the Wedge featured three dance halls with bad reputations, the roughest saloons in town, and crumbling adobe houses where prostitutes lived. Other than the notations in his memo book, Barron did not record how much money he spent in the Wedge or the names of the women he saw. However, another resident took notes on everyday life in Tucson

George Hand, Tucson saloon keeper who kept a diary recording the city's street life.

and the Wedge. His name was George Hand, and he was part owner of Foster's Saloon:

JANUARY 3, 1875. Pleasant morning. Several drunken men in town. Tom Gardner and J. B. Brown are on the warpath. Bullfight tonight at Smith's corral. Best of the season. One Mexican nearly killed. Lotteries in the evening. House full. Streets full of drunken men all night. Closed at eleven o'clock. Preaching at the courthouse today. Rosa $2. [When Hand visited a prostitute, he recorded her name and price.] MARCH 7, 1875 (SUNDAY). Very dull. Stores are all closed. My 45th birthday. Took a hot bath. Pat O'Meara got drunk, fell down, and someone stepped on his nose. Puppet show in the evening. Overstreet hit a Mexican and the Mexican hit Harrison with a stone, cutting his head. Took a walk after closing and got home at three in the morning.

Cruz $1.50.

MARCH 9. Cruz $1.50.

MARCH 16. Windy. Sober all day.

APRIL 10. Big Refugia $2.

This was Tucson in 1875, when there was one woman for every ten men. At least Barron had the decorum to write "50 cigars and perfumy" and leave it at that.

SEVEN

The Money Game

Some of the men who gathered in Lionel and Barron's store wore Levi's, frayed shirts, and leather hats stained with sweat. While the brothers were making investments and holding office in the early 1870s, these men talked about freighting to Tucson and merchants who didn't pay their transportation bills on time. Others were concerned with the cost of producing an acre of wheat and with freighters who demanded payment before hauling a load to a flour mill. Their conversations strayed to local events—a gunfight in a saloon, an upcoming hanging—but talk usually returned to what they needed the most: Money.

Like other frontier towns, Tucson didn't have much money of its own. When the military bought hay from a farmer, the farmer's money left town: he bought baling wire and plows from a merchant, and the merchant sent the money to wherever these products were manufactured. When the military bought beef from a rancher, the rancher's money left town: the rancher bought whiskey that was bottled elsewhere or barbed wire that was manufactured elsewhere. The army paid the farmer and the rancher; they paid the merchant, and the merchant sent the money to San Francisco or New York, where he had purchased the goods. With little money of their own, Tucson's businessmen needed immediate payment to stay in business—as Lionel and Barron had discovered when they lost the fourth shipment of goods and didn't have the money to cover the loss. Tucson needed money. Tucson needed its own money. By 1871, Lionel and Barron had some money, and once again one thing led to another.

Almost without thinking, they became players in what Lionel called "the money game." It started in February 1871, when Tomas Medina lost fifty head of cattle to Apaches and asked the brothers for a three-hundred-dollar loan to restock his ranch. Lionel and Barron had cash to loan because they had invested in businesses in the territory and their money hadn't left town. They granted the loan, which Barron described to Mark as "a temporary measure to help a loyal customer"—who was also Lionel's drinking buddy. Sounding defensive, Barron wrote, "Mr. Medina has a large ranch, so the money isn't really at risk." Mark let it pass, for by now his sons were doing well with their investments, and he had not forgotten Lionel's outburst.

Inevitably, other customers began asking for loans, which Barron had not anticipated but now couldn't refuse if the person was a regular customer, had collateral, and needed the cash. Lionel seemed more in favor of the loans, but Barron never mentioned this on those rare occasions when he remembered to tell Mark about the new business. By April 1871, it was clear that customers could be trusted to pay back the loans and that the brothers had found another way to make money.

It was then that Barron reported the details of the loan business to Mark and declared it "a magnificent success." They made loans of two hundred to five hundred dollars and charged 5 percent interest. They were short-term loans of thirty to sixty days, which, Barron said, "serve the purpose of keeping farmers and ranchers in business while giving us a profit." He estimated the loan business to be somewhere in the range of eight thousand dollars and declared, "Our customers have come to rely on us, and we on them to pay back the loans on time. Everyone benefits and makes money." Mark replied, "As long as customers stay loyal and you are making money, you will succeed first-rate." Barron never claimed the loan business was his idea, but Mark was left with that impression, which Barron never bothered to correct.

The other news that Barron conveyed in the early months of 1871 related to their personal lives. They had purchased horses and made it a point to go riding at least once a week to get away from business. Occasionally, if they encountered a rattlesnake, they caught it, using a stick to hold its head down, and brought it back to the Hodges Hotel, where the cook prepared it as sort of a bedtime snack. Barron related that Lionel had taken to racing horses on Sunday, and both wanted to learn to play the guitar. There were references to sharpshooting contests, horseshoe games, the Shoo Fly Café, and trips to different parts of the territory. But as one might expect, there were no references to trips to the Wedge. Otherwise it was business as usual—until the brothers pushed the money game one step further.

This time it was Barron's idea. He had come up with it in his room at the Hodges Hotel just as the loan business was showing a profit, sometime in March 1871. The brothers used a long table in Barron's room to keep track of the stacks of papers related to investments, as well as some business related to the store. As the months passed, one stack of papers kept getting higher and higher—the pile that kept track of currency exchange, when customers used the store to trade one form of money for another. "I think we might profit from a money-exchange business," Barron wrote, "and Lionel agrees."

He came up with the idea for a money-exchange business by paying attention to his customers' needs. Two forms of currency circulated in Tucson—gold coins and dollar bills, or "greenbacks," the paper money of the United States. When the military bought beef from a rancher, payment was made in greenbacks, which Lionel and Barron's customers didn't want. They didn't want greenbacks because although the government might say a greenback was worth one dollar, in reality this paper money fluctuated in value, depending on how many greenbacks the government printed, how many were in circulation in Tucson, and how much people thought they were worth. "The value of greenbacks is uncertain," Barron wrote. "They are worth sixty-five to eighty-five cents. Our customers trade greenbacks for gold because gold doesn't change in value." He asked Mark to determine the value of greenbacks in San Francisco, where the economy was more stable. When Mark reported they were worth eighty-nine cents, Barron concluded, "We might make as much as twenty-four cents on the dollar by buying greenbacks here for sixty-five cents and selling them in San Francisco for eighty-nine cents."

While Barron hatched his plan, another store was already involved in money exchange—Lord & Williams, four doors down from the Mark Jacobs Company. It dominated merchandising in Tucson. It operated a fleet of sixty freight wagons. And it was the United States depository, where the government kept its money to run the territory. But Lionel and Barron's customers needed a money-exchange service, and the brothers weren't inclined to let Lord & Williams determine their future. Besides, Lord & Williams wasn't shipping greenbacks anywhere, just exchanging them for gold. After Mark agreed to enter into the business, Lionel hung a new sign outside the store: THE MARK JACOBS COMPANY & EXCHANGE BROKERS.

Beginning in May 1871, Mark mailed two hundred dollars in gold coins to Tucson every week. They were used to buy the customers' greenbacks, which were sold at a profit in San Francisco. After two months of shipping packages back and forth, Mark wrote Barron, "The money we are making from the exchange business is gratifying. If you and Lionel agree, I am willing to increase the amount to four hundred dollars, perhaps even five hundred dollars." They agreed, and profits soared.

By the end of the year, Mark was shipping four thousand dollars a month, which brought a profit of nearly a thousand dollars. Lionel brought David Neahr in, and profits from his shipments of gold coins were split with the brothers. Gold came in from other investments in the territory, greenbacks raced out, and by 1874 Mark was shaking his head and writing, "Your idea to trade gold for greenbacks continues to amaze me. Even if Lord & Williams is depository, we will continue to prosper, with the Blessings of God, first-rate." The exchange business also benefited Tucson's economy, since the importing of gold coins eased the shortage of stable currency.

At the same time, Barron pushed the money game another step further. Besides greenbacks, he came up with the idea of buying pieces of paper that "promised" money. Perhaps half of Tucson's economy was based on these pieces of paper, which were called drafts in the 1870s; today they are known as checks. They were used instead of currency because banks in the East refused to ship real money to Tucson. The chance for robbery was too great, and the town had a bad reputation. So local businessmen established accounts in banks outside the territory and wrote "drafts" on their accounts.

The problem was that the drafts fluctuated in value as the money they were based on in banks fluctuated in value. Because it was difficult to determine the exact value of a draft, when one was accepted as payment for merchandise or a service it was "discounted"—accepted at less than face value. A draft for $500 might be accepted for a bill of $475, that is, discounted 5 percent. It might be worth more than $475, or less. To do business in Tucson, Lionel and Barron had to accept drafts from their customers, and they had to know the real value of each one. They did as well as other merchants in discounting drafts, and then Barron hit upon the idea of buying them—buying a form of money that no one wanted. This part of the business was a bit boring to Lionel, but to Barron it was absolutely exhilarating, like playing poker and winning every hand.

In an ingenious move, Barron began buying drafts with gold. Gold was always the most desired currency, and customers were glad to unload their "promised money" for gold, even at a steep discount of 10 or 15 percent. Using gold, Barron could buy a $500 draft for $450 or even $425. Then he used the draft to pay a bill of $475 or sold it for $475 in greenbacks, which were shipped to Mark to buy gold, which was shipped back to buy drafts. In the gold-for-drafts-for-greenbacks-for-gold business, the biggest customer was Lord & Williams just down the street.

It sold thousands of drafts to the brothers at discounts that averaged 12 percent, figuring it was getting the better part of the deal. Lionel did his part in keeping track of the ever more complicated money game, but at times he seemed to be a player mostly out of loyalty to his brother. He found time to learn to play the guitar, but Barron never did.

By 1874, Lionel and Barron were up late at night studying the entries in twenty-two volumes of ledgers and accounting books, if they were in town. There were books for freighting, insurance, government contracts, and branch stores. There were books for investments in Tombstone and Prescott, for the loan business, for the exchange business, and for bank accounts outside of Arizona. After eight years in Tucson, the Mark Jacobs Company was showing a steady profit from a variety of investments, and every sign indicated that all was well. Mim and the others kept writing, business was great—and Barron was in love.

By 1875, Barron had fallen in love with a young Mexican woman whose identity was a closely guarded secret. Lionel knew, but the brothers kept it from Mark because she wasn't Jewish and marriage was out of the question. When word leaked out from a relative in the territory, Mark wrote, "To say that I am disappointed understates the case. End this matter as quietly as you can." Barron replied, "I am sorry for my weakness. I was overtaken without thinking. How is it possible to control matters of the heart?" He might have added that there were no available Jewish women in Tucson.

In the evenings Barron and the girl walked in Carrillo Gardens, a series of small lakes encircled with shade trees at the south end of town. Here they embraced and shared their feelings, but

Carrillo Gardens, about 1880.

whether they ever talked about a future together isn't known. Of course Barron knew her family and knew this was forbidden love, but apparently he couldn't help it. He stopped going to the Wedge and continued the relationship with the Mexican woman in spite of Mark's disapproval.

The other event that occurred in 1875 was the end of the brothers' business relationship with their father and the end of the Mark Jacobs Company of Tucson. The prosperity of the early 1870s was accompanied by family tragedy, which led to the breakup. In February 1872, Lionel and Barron's mother had died, and Mark sank into despair. Within weeks, his daughter Julia died giving birth, and Mark's depression worsened. While still in grief Mark discovered that his son Albert had embezzled six hundred dollars from the family's businesses in San Francisco and spent the money on lavish dinners for his friends and on prostitutes. After sending Albert to Tucson "to atone for misconduct," Mark broke down completely.

Lionel traveled to San Francisco and ran the family's business for three months in 1873 until his father was well enough to resume control. From San Francisco, Lionel wrote Barron, "Pa continues easy, subject at times to fits of abstraction and vertigo which I trust he will gradually be relieved from." Perhaps Mark recovered; maybe he never did. By 1874, at the age of fifty-eight, he had fallen in love with a seventeen-year-old girl and had proposed marriage.

When the brothers heard about it from a third party, the roof almost blew off the Mark Jacobs Company. Although they were hardly examples of morality themselves, they denounced their father for bringing shame on the family and disgracing the memory of their mother. Angry letters flew back and forth and came to include all sorts of grievances. "I demand my mother's diamond earrings," Lionel thundered in one letter. Mark said no. Barron wrote that his father "lacked the sensibilities of a thinking man." Mark answered, "A son has no place to judge his father, especially considering what I have done for you."

By February 1875, Barron had assumed the role of peacemaker, but it did no good. Lionel was still ranting and calling Mark "a man with no shame or concern for his family." They decided Mark should end his connection with the firm. The agreement they negotiated denied Mark any future profits from the company. Little matter, for he had already withdrawn his investment in a huff. They gave Mark an undisclosed amount of cash as a final buyout, and on March 1, 1875, they changed the name of the business to the L. M. Jacobs Company. Mark married the seventeen-year-old girl. Lionel and Barron were on their own.

EIGHT

The Goodness of the Heart

The Arizona Social Club was a place for men to talk, read, play chess, and drink. Its spacious rooms were carpeted and furnished with expensive tables and chairs where members sat sipping brandies and liqueurs. Lionel helped establish the club early in 1875, and following the blowup with Mark, he spent most evenings there drinking Scotch whisky. The ornate oil lamps affixed to the walls flickered well into the night at the Arizona Social Club. Sometimes Lionel stayed there until three o'clock in the morning.

Lionel's withdrawal was never the main subject of Barron's letters to Mark and never presented in a negative way, as if Barron knew his brother needed a timeout. "He attends to business at midday," Barron wrote, "and has taken to hunting the desert cougar for sport, which he does in the company of other men on horseback." "Having been invited," Barron said, "Lionel joined the sheriff's posse for one ride. They were not successful as the cattle rustlers escaped to Mexico. Lionel sends his best."

It went on this way for five months until Barron devised a reconciliation with Mark, and Lionel rejoined the world. Starting in June 1875, Mark acted as "business adviser" for the L. M. Jacobs Company. He agreed never to speak the name of his new wife and to keep her out of sight whenever Lionel visited San Francisco. In the meantime Barron, at the age of twenty-nine, married Yetta, the sixteen-year-old daughter of a Jewish family in New York.

It was an arranged marriage, devised by Mark and Yetta's parents. Yetta was sent from New York shortly after Mark had learned that Barron's Mexican lover was pregnant with their child. Barron and Yetta met for the first time in June when Yetta stepped cautiously down from a stagecoach on Main Street. Wearing braided hair and a long dress with a high collar, Yetta was a no-nonsense woman, who even at sixteen knew exactly what she was getting in Barron Jacobs: a Jewish husband of means and social standing. Mark didn't attend the wedding, and the only advice he gave to Barron was, "Be faithful to your wife." Mark never mentioned love, and Barron made no mention of the ceremony.

After the wedding, Barron stopped seeing the Mexican woman. It wasn't clear how much Yetta knew about her, but she quickly sized up the situation and was a partner in establishing an allowance and in making plans for the education of Barron's child. Yetta became active in social affairs and in designing their new home, which was soon under construction. She assumed her status as the wife of a prosperous merchant easily and gracefully, and Barron always spoke well of her. "Yetta has learned to prepare Mexican dishes," he said. "Yetta gets on well as our bookkeeper and delights in reminding us of our mistakes," he said. Barron never spoke of love when he mentioned Yetta, but he probably grew to love her, and she him.

Solving the family's personal problems came at a fortunate time, for new business opportunities were opening in southern Arizona. Tucson was changing. In 1875, a telegraph line linked the town to the outside world. In 1877, a daily mail service to California began. The Southern Pacific Railroad Corporation was building a line from San Diego to Tucson, and it was predicted to reach Tucson by 1880, reducing shipping costs for merchants and creating new opportunities for businessmen.

At the same time, a string of dizzying events revealed that Arizona wasn't so forsaken after all. In 1877, a silver strike near Prescott caused the town's population to triple in less than a month. The territorial capital was relocated back to Prescott, but it didn't matter. In the same year an even richer vein of silver was discovered at Tombstone in southeastern Arizona, and Tucson became headquarters for southern Arizona's extensive mining operations. Like lightning striking the territory, other discoveries of gold, silver, and copper were made in Globe, Bisbee, Clarkdale, Jerome, Superior, Ajo, and Morenci. In 1870, Arizona mined $800,000 in precious metals. In 1882, it mined $11 million in precious metals.

The discoveries attracted outside capital, which transformed the territory's economy. The cattle business was booming. The farming business was booming. The merchandising business was booming. Nearly every business was booming—from freighting to the mines to quenching the thirst of the miners, who put a strain on Tucson's many, many saloons. The Wedge was booming. Between 1870 and 1880, the territory's non-native population increased from 9,658 to 40,440, a gain of 318 percent. Now Tucson had some money of its own. But it was in need of something else at the time that Mark reconciled with his sons. Tucson needed a bank.

In contrast to other business ventures, Lionel and Barron resisted the idea of starting a bank. The subject first came up in August 1875, when Lionel suggested it as "a matter for debate and not necessarily a good idea." As if he had found new life, Lionel joined in the correspondence with Mark and took the lead in discussing the idea, which he called "foolish" and "dangerous," or "wise" and "worthwhile," depending on whether he was arguing pro or con. All three saw the need for a bank in southern Arizona—and the risk of losing everything if things went bad.

On the positive side, the brothers had been bankers, sort of, for at least five years, as Lionel noted. They knew who could be trusted with a loan and who couldn't. They knew the value of a crop offered as collateral. They knew the money-exchange business. For years the safe in their store had served as a secure place for their customers' money, but they had never taken a "deposit" of money in which they paid the customer interest. A few things were clear about starting a bank, Lionel said: "We would need a vault, not a safe, and a lot of money, which means taking in partners."

On the negative side, there was Lord & Williams. Although not legally incorporated as a bank, Lord & Williams had most of Tucson's money and was considered the town's "official bank." It remained the United States depository for Arizona Territory, even after the capital went back to Prescott. Lionel and Barron had always lived in the shadow of the giant firm, and they had seen four of the eight stores in town go under in trying to compete with Lord & Williams. Lionel called the company a sleeping giant, but he often emphasized the word "sleeping." "If the Tombstone mines continue producing silver," he said, the bank would be a good idea. "If the economy continues to grow," he said, the bank would be a good idea. "If Lord & Williams doesn't open a bank first and use its wealth to monopolize the economy," the bank would be a good idea. If, if, if.

Upon the advice of Mark to go slow, in October 1875, Lionel and Barron began offering longer-term loans of a thousand dollars for a year to trusted customers. They were the only ones in town who offered long-term loans, and soon their customers were asking for even larger amounts, proving the need for a bank but putting the brothers in a tough position. Barron wrote, "The demand for investment capital is greater than we anticipated and I fear we will be cash short in a matter of months." Lionel wrote, "Lord & Williams still doesn't act while our customers want money, money, and more money." By March 1876, Lionel was reading books on banking and studying the National Banking Act of 1863, which regulated banking operations in the United States.

The next step came in April 1876, when the brothers quietly remodeled one of the storage rooms located at the back of their store. They hired a carpenter to knock down the wall facing into the store so patrons could easily enter the 10-by-12-foot room. The carpenter worked behind a curtain, and after two weeks the room had a counter, a banister, red carpeting, and paneling on its ceiling and walls. Before the curtain was removed, Lionel and Barron placed three 3-by-5-foot safes behind the counter and filled them with their money, their customers' money, and the financial records of their customers. The place looked like a bank, but there was not even a tiny sign saying BANK.

Customers knew what went on in this room, and as Arizona's economy grew, more people crowded into the area with red carpet. Normally both brothers tended the counter, while the merchandising part of the business was left to relatives and Yetta, who assumed the position of leader whenever she worked in the store. Quietly Lionel and Barron began accepting deposits of money ranging from five dollars to thousands of dollars. In return they issued deposit slips that specified the amount in the account and the rate of interest, 3 percent. As the Tombstone mines produced more silver and gold, more money poured in as savings at 3 percent, and more poured out as loans at 5 percent.

The bank that didn't say it was a bank met the needs of Lionel and Barron's customers. And the bond between the brothers and their customers grew as their customers' businesses grew. In June 1876, Henry Hooker, who had helped the brothers win a beef contract, walked out of the "store" with $5,500 to expand his Sierra Bonita Ranch. In October, James Brash, who owned a flour mill in Florence, walked out with $7,000. In 1877, the brothers loaned $6,000 to the Territory of Arizona and $14,000 to Pima County. Customers wore a path in the red carpet while Lord & Williams was busy selling boots and axle grease.

By September 1878, Lionel had mastered the banking codes, and he and Barron had devised a plan to open a formal bank in the store. It called for an investment of $50,000 in cash. The brothers had raised $25,000, which was, as Lionel put it, "virtually all the money we have that isn't invested in merchandise or loans." They intended to invest all of it and to find partners who would let them control the bank. In today's terms, the $25,000 was roughly equivalent to $200,000, and the brothers were ready to bet it all on three things: one, the Tombstone mines wouldn't peter out; two, no one else would open a bank first; and three, if there was a competing bank, customers would remain loyal to them and use their bank. As booming as it was, Tucson's economy probably couldn't support two banks and certainly not three. Tucson needed one bank. In October, Lionel and Barron decided to take their biggest gamble and began searching for partners. Neither anticipated the next event.

On November 30, 1878, Tucson's *Arizona Weekly Citizen* announced that the town was about to get its first bank, but it was not Lionel and Barron's bank. In searching for investors, the brothers had approached several wealthy residents as likely partners. But word of the brothers' initiative leaked out, and it was hijacked. The newspaper announced that four of the most powerful men in Tucson had formed a partnership and would open a bank as soon as they could consolidate their funds, acquire a building, and secure a safe and needed equipment. In other words, all they had was an idea for starting a bank. They were former territorial governor Anson Safford, Tucson mayor James Toole, former newspaper editor John Wasson, and local businessman Charles Hudson. Lionel and Barron knew these men and considered them friends. So much for friends in high places.

Barron wrote only one letter to Mark about being upstaged. He and Lionel discussed "other courses of action" and concluded that they should invest the $25,000 in the Safford bank. "But when we approached Mr. Safford and Mr. Toole and made our proposal," Barron wrote, "it was made clear to us that the venture was purely a white concern, excluding Jews and Mexicans." Staying restrained as usual, Barron said, "We've done business with them, in joint investments. We've dined together. Yetta is best friends with Mr. Toole's wife." It hurt more than this, but it wasn't in Barron to say how much. Lionel didn't comment at all, which was just as well. Barron told Mark that they were resuming their search for investors, mainly because Lionel pointed out that the Safford group didn't know the banking codes, didn't have a building, and didn't have a safe. He might have added, "or a conscience."

Within a few weeks, Lionel and Barron had the other $25,000. They were joined by four close friends who had been customers for years and who also had an eye for profit. They were E. B. Gage, owner of the Grand Central Mine in Tombstone; Pinckney Tully, a Hispanic and co-owner of Tully & Ochoa, the third-largest merchandising firm in Tucson; Phillip Smith, owner of the Vulture Mine in central Arizona; and A. Lazard, the Jewish lawyer who had sold his store to the brothers in 1872.

Whether the Safford group knew it or not, they couldn't just start a bank. They needed authorization, which meant knowing how to apply and knowing the banking codes. Now Lionel used his expertise to his and Barron's advantage. On December 24, 1878, he filed articles of incorporation for the Pima County Bank. The articles sought authorization for banking transactions at the Tucson office and at any branch office the partners might establish in the future. The articles were granted, and on January 1, 1879, the Pima County Bank opened its doors, the first bank in Tucson. Lionel nailed another sign below the one outside the store:

L. M. JACOBS COMPANY

PIMA COUNTY BANK

What followed was an undeclared banking war with winner take all. By the summer of 1879, both Lord & Williams and the

Safford partnership had started banks. Swiftly Lionel and Barron remodeled their store again so that half the space was devoted to banking. A floor-to-ceiling partition cut the store in half, and a wide entranceway was used to get from the merchandising half to the banking half, where the red carpet started. First Lionel, then Barron, was elected cashier and given control of the bank. Now the bet was on the loyalty of their customers.

They did not let the brothers down. On a typical day both halves of the store were filled with people of fairness and good will, with people who had seen the brothers help build the community, serve in office, and donate money to charities and the like. It was their loyalty that won Tucson's banking war for Lionel and Barron. In 1881, a rumor spread that Lord & Williams faced bankruptcy because it had overextended its operations. Its customers made a run on the bank, and people feared that the giant firm's collapse would affect other banks. But there was no run on the Pima County Bank, and it was business as usual.

In October 1881, Lord & Williams declared bankruptcy and went out of business; it didn't have enough customers to be a bank. In 1884, the Safford bank declared bankruptcy and went out of business; it didn't have enough customers either. Tucson needed one bank and it chose Lionel and Barron's. It was a victory for the frontier values of hard work and the need for fairness.

NINE

The Goodness of Life

On March 19, 1880, the Southern Pacific Railroad reached Tucson. If ever the town needed a reason for cork-popping and celebrating, this was it. Mayor Robert Leatherwood hosted the event and drank toast after toast with the cheering crowd, which numbered in the thousands and was louder than any train could be. An old tale passed down through time had it that Leatherwood sent a telegram to the Pope in Rome asking for a blessing to be read when the first train arrived. The Pope complied, and as the first train rolled in, a local priest read the blessing aloud, including the sentence that followed the blessing: *"Where in hell is Tucson?"*

Lost among the toasts to growth and prosperity was another consequence of the arrival of the railroad: the final defeat of the Apache Nation. The railroad brought new settlers to southern Arizona. New farms and ranches, new roads and communities pushed the Apaches farther off their land. They fought back with a vengeance in the 1880s, until they could fight no more.

Pushed into the Sierra Madres of northern Mexico, Geronimo led his warriors on raids into Arizona from 1876 to 1886 until his band was down to forty-two warriors and ninety women and children. They faced two thousand troops commanded by General

George Crook, who was under intense pressure from settlers to finish Geronimo once and for all. Crook hesitated. Like many frontier generals, he knew Native Americans better than most whites and sympathized with their cause. Known as the "humanitarian general," Crook spoke out against the injustice of America's Indian policy. He stalled, allowing Geronimo to raid ranches and steal cattle to keep his band alive. Geronimo and the last of the Apaches finally surrendered in March 1886. There was a sullen peace.

The defeat of the Apaches and the arrival of the railroad didn't mean that Arizona was suddenly "civilized"; savagery was still plentiful. Headed by Doc Holliday, "Old Man" Clanton, and John Ringo, gangs of cattle rustlers, operating near Tombstone, stole livestock and killed ranchers when they gave chase. Billy the Kid drifted in and out of the territory, usually when he was wanted for murder in New Mexico. The Black Canyon stage, running from Phoenix to Prescott, was robbed on January 13, April 21, June 1, and October 18, 1884. The Wells Fargo stage was robbed so many times that the famous frontier marshal Wyatt Earp was hired as a guard. After he and his brothers killed a gang of bandits in what witnesses said was cold-blooded murder, the Earps were brought to trial; they were set free. Tombstone had four robberies, five shootings, and eight killings in three months in 1884.

Citizens pitched in by hanging "suspected" criminals without a trial. On August 3, 1882, the town of Globe featured two hangings of suspected murderers. On December 9, Bisbee hanged a suspected thief, and on March 28, 1884, it boasted five hangings of suspected bandits. Holbrook had a double hanging in 1885, witnessed by a crowd in the hundreds, many of whom were drunk. Flagstaff had a double hanging in 1887, with the same kind of crowd. When he wasn't writing about his trips to the Wedge, George Hand recorded other news:

> OCTOBER 9, 1882. Fine morning. Two men dead. One natural death, the other named Hewitt, was beat till he died.
>
> NOVEMBER 1. Man killed last night.
>
> NOVEMBER 2. Chinaman got a bad beating this morning.
>
> NOVEMBER 7. A row occurred at the Park Theater. Alex Levin tried to stop it and got two bad cuts on his head. John Dobbs got knocked under the table. Several others beaten by the railroaders. No one killed.
>
> JANUARY 1, 1883. White, jailer, opened cell door. Two prisoners jumped out and gave him a terrible beating and escaped. Sheriff Paul is red hot.
>
> JANUARY 17. Paul took a prisoner to the hospital today. He was shot while robbing a man five days ago. Both elbows and hands broken and shattered badly. He will not steal again for a long time.
>
> MARCH 3. Some son of a gun came in my room and appropriated a pound of fine cut tobacco, leaving me without a chew. That was very unkind.

While Tucson staggered through the 1880s, Lionel and Barron continued running the Pima County Bank, but the arrival of the railroad changed the business of merchandising in Tucson. Orders for merchandise from San Francisco, and later Kansas City, could be sent in minutes by telegraph and received in days

Lionel M. Jacobs.

by train. Starting in 1880, prices on practically all merchandise in Tucson fell because transportation costs fell. Many of the old firms were caught with expensive stock, while inexpensive new goods arrived by train. A. & L. Zeckendorf tried to survive by discounting its merchandise and using increased sales to recover the loss; it went bankrupt in 1883. Tully & Ochoa had tried the same thing; it went bankrupt in 1882.

As the railroad approached Tucson, Lionel and Barron were at odds over what to do. Barron wrote that he was "strongly in favor of getting out of the business of selling altogether." "Lionel," Barron said, "thinks we should hang on for a while longer and not spread ourselves thin." Apparently, for the first time, Barron held firm in an argument with his brother, although

Barron M. Jacobs.

it isn't clear how hard Lionel argued back. "He is wrong," Barron wrote Mark, "but he will see the light if I have anything to do with it." It didn't help that Yetta sided with Lionel, except that it made Barron more stubborn: "She thinks she knows what she is talking about, notwithstanding the completion of the railroad to Tucson." It was good that Barron kept arguing.

Emphasizing the booming Tombstone mines and the need for expanded banking services, Barron eventually won the argument, or Lionel let him win. In any case, the brothers got out of the merchandising business in February 1880—three weeks before the arrival of the railroad. They left merchandising to Lord & Williams at exactly the right moment—when it became unprofitable. Still snoozing, Lord & Williams was caught with a huge

Henrietta "Yetta" Jacobs, photographed about 1900.

inventory of goods it couldn't unload. It went bankrupt in 1882, shortly after its bank collapsed. Of the eight merchants in Tucson when Lionel and Barron arrived in 1867, Lord & Williams was the seventh to declare bankruptcy. The eighth, A. Lazard, had sold out to Lionel and Barron in 1872 and left the business voluntarily. New businesses bringing goods to Tucson by more modern methods had taken the place of the frontier merchant.

After they sold their stock of goods at auction, Lionel and Barron tore down the partition separating their two businesses and remodeled the entire store in wall-to-wall red carpet. Thereafter, the new Pima County Bank did everything the old bank did but on a much larger scale. By 1885, it had the appearance of a modern bank, with eight tellers and separate desks in other areas for loan officers, property assessments, and new accounts. It had a vault in a separate room where much of southern Arizona's wealth was kept. Customers, some of whom had known Lionel and Barron for nearly twenty years, waited in long lines for service. They were happy to do so because the brothers could still be counted on when times were hard, or good. The bank prospered throughout the 1880s and 1890s.

By 1885, day-to-day operations were turned over to other family members. Lionel and Barron came in for a few hours in the morning or afternoon to approve loans in the $20,000 range and offer business advice to customers, who were glad to get it. Increasingly the brothers devoted much of their time to improving Tucson society.

Both sat on the sanitation committee and oversaw the cleaning of Mesilla Street and the others. Both were charter members of the Tucson Literary Society. It met on Friday evenings at a member's home. Women were active participants in the organization. Along with Lionel and Barron, Yetta read passages from the book of the week and was firm in holding her opinion of an author in the discussions, which often became heated. With other women she helped raise money to start Tucson's first public library. With Lionel and Barron she worked to establish Tucson's school system.

In 1886, Lionel helped establish the Owls Club, an exclusive boarding establishment for unattached men. It did not discriminate on the basis of race or religion and its members were drawn from the top of society. They spent much of their time giving parties where the dress was elegant, the music refined, and the dancing graceful and delicate. Lionel was always in demand by the women attending the masked balls and soirees, which were the talk of the town. Tucsonans vied for invitations to the dances and the elegant dinners where the men and their guests savored oysters on the half-shell, champagne, and French desserts prepared by the club's gifted Chinese cook, Woo Sing.

Grace and beauty came to Tucson whenever the Owls Club put on an event, and Lionel was always in the middle of it as an organizer and participant. He was also one of the club's top debaters. For an hour or more he would debate a subject such as "overproduction and underconsumption of merchandise," and he would switch back and forth, debating both sides of the issue. He was known to stop in the middle of a sentence and say, "Just a minute," before switching to the other side.

Lionel's trips to San Francisco continued, although now they were more frequent and of longer duration. When he visited the city, he stayed at the expensive Lick House for months at a time, during which, according to a newspaper, he enjoyed "the sweet pleasures of bachelor life." "He sleeps at the Lick House and eats only the finest foods while entertaining female acquaintances," the reporter wrote, as if it were big news. Lionel still saw Mimmie. He still saw the others and made new "acquaintances." As late as 1889, a local newspaper was reporting the rumor, "L. M. Jacobs to be married to wealthy woman in San Francisco." It wasn't even close to the truth. Surely he broke a hundred hearts of those who were not cautious in love.

Barron and Yetta toured Europe in the 1880s and again in the 1890s, and used the trips to acquire furnishings for their imposing two-story Victorian home. Lionel, Barron, and Yetta held

Barron and Yetta's home, across the street from Tucson's Presbyterian Church, about 1885.

seats on the select Committee of Invitation, which sponsored the most important social parties in Tucson, many of which took place in Yetta's home with Yetta as hostess. Customers, business associates, Owls Club members, and unattached women sat at the long dining table with eight high-backed chairs on each side. They were served by Jewish and Hispanic girls wearing white dresses and bonnets with crimson trim.

Barron sat at one end of the table, Yetta at the other, and Lionel might be seated anywhere, depending on the company. These were long dinner parties where friends shared the rewards of successful lives. Embossed in gold-leaf script on a background of pure silk, one dinner invitation read as follows:

SOUP: *Tomato with rice*
FISH: *Salmon with anchovy sauce*
MEATS: *Roast turkey with cranberry and apple sauce*
Roast beef and sweetbreads with mushrooms
Chicken fricassee
SALADS: *Shrimp and chicken salad, and tomato*
VEGETABLES: *Green peas, cabbage, asparagus, string beans with*
tomato sauce
POTATOES: *Fried, boiled, and mashed*
DESSERT: *Plum pudding with cream sauce, cake and ice cream*
WINES: *White wine, claret, and champagne*
COFFEE AND TEA, FRUIT

It was a long way from hardtack and beans.

When the dust settled on the American West in the 1890s, about the time the brothers were giving expensive dinner parties, the merchant-banker seemed more notable than other frontier types. The Indian fighter disappeared with the end of the Indian wars. The heyday of the mountain man ended when the beaver and otter in the West, once plentiful, became too scarce to hunt. The gold rush prospector stayed in the West or returned home, most often penniless.

Meanwhile, the Pima County Bank evolved into the First National Bank, the Bank of Tucson, the Consolidated Bank of Tucson, and the present Valley National Bank, of which there are currently 190 branches throughout Arizona.

"The Wedge" district of downtown Tucson at the end of the nineteenth century. The corner building on the left is the First National Bank—successor to Lionel and Barron Jacobs's Pima County Bank.

Afterword

David Neahr married Maria Hupohauss, a beautiful woman of the Cocopah culture. They had ten children. In addition to being a forwarding agent, Neahr operated a cattle ranch near Yuma, where he won the trust of Native American peoples living along the Colorado River. Each spring the Cocopah and other groups gathered at Neahr's ranch to prepare for their annual deer hunt. Neahr gave them a couple of his best cattle for their feast of thanks and gave them meat, flour, and coffee to sustain them during the hunt.

In the late nineteenth century, whites joined various Native American groups in their struggle to get their land back. The Indian Rights Association and the Sequoya League lobbied Congress for action, but it was not until 1946 that Congress created the Indians Claims Commission for settling land disputes with Native Americans. By 1978, the commission had settled more than two hundred claims for a total of $800 million. The Apaches were granted land in New Mexico and Arizona. Like other Native Americans, they reached their low point in population around 1915, when they numbered less than 3,000. Since then their numbers have been on the rise, and in 1990 there were 50,051 Apaches. Native Americans were made citizens of the United States in 1924.

Albert Jacobs, Lionel and Barron's younger brother who had embezzled money from Mark, became a successful merchant in Safford and Tucson. In 1883, he helped establish the Jewish organization B'nai B'rith in Arizona and was elected its first president. Selmin Franklin, son of Lionel and Barron's sister Victoria, clerked in the Tucson store until 1877, when Lionel and Barron sent him to the University of California. After graduating, Selmin returned to Tucson, where he became a prominent political figure. He was city attorney and assistant U.S. attorney, and after being elected to the Arizona legislature, he introduced the bill establishing the University of Arizona in Tucson. Selmin Franklin became known as the father of the University of Arizona, now one of the leading state universities in the nation.

Mark Jacobs stayed married to his second wife and continued to act as a business adviser to Lionel and Barron until his death in 1894. Although he and his sons were friendly toward one another, Lionel never did meet his father's second wife. At the time of his death, Mark was seventy-eight. He was survived by more than sixty grandchildren, including Barron's child by the Mexican girl, of whom history has left no record.

Barron and Yetta had one child, Hilda, who was born in 1877. Hilda was a member of the first graduating class of the University of Arizona. She married Brigadier General Charles Drake, the commander of the U.S. Army at Fort Lowell. Soon after the wedding, Hilda accompanied her husband to the Philippines, where he fought in the Spanish-American War.

During the 1880s, Lionel and Barron were instrumental in building a water system for Tucson, and by the end of the decade most houses had piped water and gaslights. In the 1890s, Lionel was elected chairman of the powerful Democratic Territorial Committee, and he also served on a committee lobbying Congress for statehood. In 1903, the brothers helped form the Arizona Bankers' Association to promote manufacturing in Arizona, and in 1906, with Yetta, they supervised the raising of

money in Arizona for the victims of the San Francisco earth-
quake.

Arizona continued to grow because of its rich copper mines. In
1910 it had a population of 204,000, and in 1912 it was admit-
ted as the forty-eighth state. Lionel and Barron retired from business in 1912. The Jacobs family retained control of the Pima
County Bank until 1935.

Upon retirement, both brothers stayed in Tucson. Barron and
Yetta continued to travel abroad until Barron's ill health caused
them to move to Washington, D.C., where they lived with their
daughter and her family. Barron died in 1936 at the age of ninety.
Yetta died in 1951 at the age of ninety-two.

In 1910, two years before he retired, Lionel married Bertha
Frank, the daughter of a Jewish family in New York. Lionel was
seventy and Bertha thirty-eight. At his retirement ceremony
sponsored by the Arizona Bankers' Association, Lionel remi-
nisced about the trip to Tucson in 1867 and recalled merchandising in frontier Arizona. Still skillful at public speaking, he
spoke with a measured delivery but showed enthusiasm when he
discussed "the new machinery" that would make work easier and
change communications. The typewriter and telephone, he said
in 1912, would open the door to unlimited business opportunities. Lionel died in Tucson in 1922 at the age of eighty-two.
Nearly a thousand people attended his funeral.

By 1912, Lionel and Barron had held more than a dozen different offices, and their personal wealth was equal to more than
$3 million in current money. In 1845, fewer than twenty thou-
sand whites lived in the two-million-square-mile area west of
Kansas. By 1890, the area had a population of more than three

million and today has more than forty million. In 1867, Arizona had a non-native population of less than seven thousand. Today it has reached the four-million mark and Tucson has reached half a million.

Starting in 1878, a sanitation service kept Mesilla Street and the downtown district clean. After the railroad reached the frontier towns, wagon freighting diminished and the nigh and his mates ended their work, barely remembered in the story of the settlement of the West. The Shoo Fly Café closed in 1882.

Bibliographic Note

Information concerning the role of Jews in gold rush California and the West came from the following sources: Rudolph Glanz, *The Jews of California from the Discovery of Gold Until 1880* (New York: Walden Press, 1960); Kenneth and Irving Howe, *We Lived There Too: In Their Own Words and Pictures—Pioneer Jews and the Westward Movement of America, 1630–1900* (New York: St. Martin's Press, 1984); Robert E. Levinson, "American Jews in the West," *Western Historical Quarterly* (July 1974), 285–294; Robert E. Levinson, *The Jews of the California Gold Rush* (New York: Ktav Publishing House, 1978); Irena Narell, *Our City: The Jews of San Francisco* (San Diego: Howell-North, 1980); Moses Rischin, ed., *The Jews of the West: The Metropolitan Years* (Waltham, Mass.: American Jewish Historical Society, 1979); Harriet and Fred Rochlin, *Pioneer Jews: A New Life in the Far West* (Boston: Houghton Mifflin Co., 1984); I. Harold Sharfman, *Jews on the Frontier* (Chicago: Henry Regnery Co., 1977); and Elizabeth Van Steenwyk, *Levi Strauss: The Blue Jeans Man* (New York: Walker and Company, 1988).

For general information on the history of the West and Southwest, see Ray Allen Billington, *The Far Western Frontier, 1830–1860* (New York: Harper & Row, 1956); J. Ross Browne, *Adventures in the Apache Country: A Tour Through Arizona and Sonora* (New York: Promontory Press, 1974); and Lynn I. Perrigo, *The American Southwest: Its Peoples and Cultures* (New York: Holt, Rinehart and Winston, 1971).

For the early history of Tucson, see Clement Eaton, "Frontier Life in Southern Arizona," *Southwestern Historical Quarterly*

(January 1933), 172–192; John Bret Hart, *Tucson: Portrait of a Desert Pueblo* (Woodland Hills, Calif.: Windsor Publications, Inc., 1980); Madeline Ferrin Pare, *Arizona Pageant: A Short History of the 48th State* (Phoenix: Arizona Historical Foundation, 1965); Thomas H. Peterson, Jr., "A Tour of Tucson—1874," *Journal of Arizona History* (Autumn 1970), 180–201; Margaret K. Purcell, "Life and Leisure in Tucson Before 1880" (Master's thesis, University of Arizona, 1969); and Charles L. Sonnichsen, *Tucson: The Life and Times of an American City* (Norman, Okla.: University of Oklahoma Press, 1982).

For the Apache Nation and the Apache wars, see Odie B. Faulk, *Crimson Desert: Indian Wars of the American Southwest* (New York: Oxford University Press, 1974); Charles L. Sonnichsen, *The Mescalero Apaches* (Norman, Okla.: University of Oklahoma Press, 1959); and Edward H. Spicer, *Cycles of Conquest: The Impact of Spain, Mexico and the United States on the Indians of the Southwest, 1533–1960* (Tucson: University of Arizona Press, 1962).

The following sources provided information on merchandising in the West: Lewis B. Atherton, *The Frontier Merchant in Mid-America* (Columbia, Mo.: University of Missouri Press, 1971); Floyd S. Fierman, "Peddlers and Merchants on the Southwest Frontier, 1850–1880," *Passward* (Spring 1963), 43–55; Josiah Gregg, *Commerce of the Prairies* (Norman, Okla.: University of Oklahoma Press, 1954); Leon Harris, *Merchant Princes: An Intimate History of Jewish Families Who Built Great Department Stores* (New York: Harper & Row, 1979); and Penrose Scull, *From Peddlers to Merchant Princes: A History of Selling in America* (New York: Follett Publishing Company, 1967).

The following sources provided information on transportation in the West: Harry S. Drago, *The Steamboaters* (New York: Dodd, Mead and Company, 1967); James R. Jennings, *The Freight Rolled* (San Antonio, Tex.: Naylor Company, 1969); Henry P. Walker, "Freighting from Guaymas to Tucson, 1850–1880," *Western Historical Quarterly* (July 1970), 291–304; and Henry P. Walker, *The Wagonmasters: High Plains Freighting from the Earliest Days of the Santa Fe Trail to 1880* (Norman, Okla.: University of Oklahoma Press, 1966).

Information on Jewish merchants and bankers in the West and the Jacobs family came from Lamb Blaine, "Pioneer Jews in Arizona, 1852–1920" (Ph.D. dissertation, Arizona State University, 1982); Don C. Bridenstine, "Commercial Banking in Arizona—Past and Present" (Ph.D. dissertation, University of Southern California, 1958); Richard L. and Arlene A. Golden, "The Mark I. Jacobs Family: A Discursive Overview," *Western States Jewish Historical Quarterly* (January 1981), 99–114; Chuck Hermann, "When Bankers Wore Boots," *Arizona Highways* (September 1977); Dawn Moore, "The Banking Operations of Lionel and Barron Jacobs in Tucson, Arizona, 1867–1913" (Master's thesis, University of Arizona, 1988); Dawn Moore, "Pioneer Banking in Tucson: Lionel and Barron Jacobs and the Founding of the Pima County Bank," *Arizona and the West* (1982), 305–318; Dawn Moore Santiago, "The Owls Club of Tucson," *Journal of Arizona History* (1992), 241–268; Harriet Rochlin, "Enterprising People: Pioneer Jews of Arizona," *Arizona Past* (September 1980); Gerald Stanley, "Merchandising in the Southwest: The Mark I. Jacobs Company of Tucson, 1867 to 1875," *American Jewish Archives* (April 1971), 86–102; Norton B. Stern, "Bad Day at San Bernardino,"

Western States Jewish Historical Quarterly (October 1974), 61–66.

The most valuable source for primary information, including Barron's letters, is the Jacobs family papers in Special Collections, University of Arizona (22 boxes of manuscript materials and 177 volumes of business records) and in the Arizona Historical Society's Barron & Lionel Jacobs Collection (4,200 items).

University of Arizona archivists Roger Myers and Laura Morgan provided helpful assistance in locating materials in the Jacobs family papers and Gayle Willer facilitated research at the Arizona Historical Society in Tucson. The author is grateful to the University of Arizona and the Arizona Historical Society for granting permission to quote materials from the collections. Robin Tidmore provided additional research on David Neahr. Some quotations were edited for clarity.

Index

Apaches, 21, 22, 23, 24, 37, 41, 42, 46, 53-56, 62, 79, 80, 90
Arizona Territory, 10, 11, 72, 79, 80, 92, 93
  becomes state, 92
  creation of, 21, 23

Browne, J. Ross, 26

California gold rush, 1-4
  Jews in, 3-4
Camp Grant massacre, 55-56
Carson, Kit, 23, 24, 54
Cochise, 23
Crook, Gen. George, 79-80

drafts, 65-66, 67
Drake, Brig. Gen. Charles, 91
Drake, Hilda (Jacobs), 91

Earp, Wyatt, 80

Franklin, Abraham, 56-57
Franklin, Selmin, 90-91
Franklin, Victoria (Jacobs), 90

Geronimo, 23, 79, 80
Gila Trail, the, 12-20, 21, 32
greenbacks, 64, 65

Hand, George, 59-60, 81

Jacobs, Albert, 57, 68, 90
Jacobs, Barron:
  arrival in Tucson, 25-27
  becomes frontier merchant, 10, 11
  begins "money game," 62-66
  childhood of, 7-8
  civic works of, 85, 91-92
  daughter of, see Drake, Hilda (Jacobs)
  death of, 92
  described, 8
  early days in business, 29-31, 33-34
  falls in love, 67-68
  gambling of, 48
  journey to Tucson, 12-14, 16-17, 18-20, 25-26
  marries Yetta, 71
  relations with Lionel, 7, 69, 70

Jacobs, Barron (cont.)
  relations with Mark, 67, 69, 70-71
  relations with townsfolk, 47-50, 85, 87-88
  retirement of, 92
  visits to the Wedge, 58, 60
Jacobs, Bertha (Frank), 92
Jacobs, Hannah (Soloman), 5, 68
Jacobs, Henrietta "Yetta," 71, 72, 75, 83, 84, 85, 86, 87, 91, 92
Jacobs, Julia, 68
Jacobs, Leah, 6
Jacobs, Lionel:
  and transportation problem, 34-35, 40, 41
  becomes frontier merchant, 10, 11
  childhood of, 5-6
  death of, 92
  described, 6
  early days in business, 29-31, 33
  fighting of, 48
  journey to Tucson, 12-14, 16, 17, 18-20, 25-26
  learns banking codes, 74, 75
  marries Bertha Frank, 92
  public service of, 53-54, 56, 70, 85, 91-92
  relations with Barron, 7, 69, 70
  relations with Mark, 40, 52, 69, 70-71, 91
  relations with townsfolk, 47-50
  relations with women, 9, 57-58, 86, 92
  retirement of, 92
Jacobs, Mark Israel, 5, 6, 8, 10, 31-32, 33, 34, 39-40, 51, 52, 53, 54, 62, 63, 67, 68-69, 70-71, 72, 73, 91
  relationship with sons, 6, 9, 51-52, 67, 68-69, 70-71, 74
Jews:
  as pioneers, 3-4
  prejudice against, 7-8

Lazard, A., 53, 77, 84
Lord & Williams, 26, 27, 28, 30, 53, 64, 65, 66, 73, 74, 75, 77, 78, 83-84

mescal beans, 26
mule skinners, 37-38
mules, 38, 39

Neahr, David, 35, 36, 37, 40, 65, 90
nigh, 39

Pennington, Larcena, 54-55
Pima County Bank, 77, 78, 81, 84, 88,
  89, 92

Shoo Fly Café, the, 49-50, 53, 63, 93
Sonoran Desert, 14-19
Southern Pacific Railroad, 72
span, 38, 39

"Sunday laws," 8

Tucson, 10, 11, 18, 19-20, 21, 22-25,
  26-27, 30, 31, 41-42, 51, 71-72, 79,
  91-92, 93
  described, 26-27
  founding of, 22-25

Wallen, Mrs. Florence, 49, 50
Wedge, the, 58, 59, 63, 68, 72, 89
wheelers, 38

Jerry Stanley is the author of *Children of the Dust Bowl: The True Story of the School at Weedpatch Camp*, which was named a Notable Book for Children by the American Library Association and received several distinguished children's book awards, including the Orbis Pictus Award, the California Library Association's John and Patricia Beatty Award, and the Virginia Library Association's Jefferson Cup. His other books for young readers are *I Am an American: A True Story of Japanese Internment* and *Big Annie of Calumet: A True Story of the Industrial Revolution*, both also American Library Association Notable Books for Children, and *Digger: The Tragic Fate of the California Indians from the Missions to the Gold Rush*.

Jerry Stanley received his master's degree and Ph.D. from the University of Arizona, and was professor of history at California State University at Bakersfield until 1998, when he retired to become a full-time writer. He lives in Bakersfield with his wife, Dorothy.